The
SHERLOCK
HOLMES
Puzzle Collection

Published by SevenOaks

an imprint of Carlton Publishing Group
20 Mortimer Street
London W1T 3JW

ISBN 978-1-86200-872-4

Project editor: Richard Wolfrik Galland
Text and puzzles: Tim Dedopulos
Design: James Pople
Production: Dawn Cameron

⚬—◦

Full-page original artworks: Rebecca Wright
Additional art and watercolouring: Chris Gould

The publishers would like to thank Mary Evans Picture Library for their kind permission to reproduce the pictures in this book which appear on the following pages:

10, 14, 16, 23, 27, 30, 40, 41, 43, 44, 49, 54, 55, 57, 59, 60, 61, 62, 63, 64, 65, 66, 70, 74, 75, 76, 79, 83, 84, 85, 86, 89, 90, 92, 94, 96, 97, 99, 100. 101, 106, 107, 108, 109, 110, 113, 115, 117, 120, 122, 123, 124, 126, 127, 128, 129, 130, 136, 137, 138, 139, 140, 141, 145, 151, 153, 154, 155, 158, 159, 160, 161, 162, 163, 164, 168, 171, 176, 178, 207, 210, 213, 217, 218, 221, 223, 227, 230, 233, 235, 238, 245, 248, 250, 258, 263, 264, 267, 275 & 277

Every effort has been made to acknowledge correctly and contact the source and/or copyright holder of each picture and Carlton Books Limited apologises for any unintentional errors or omissions, which will be corrected in future editions of this book.

Printed in China

The
SHERLOCK
HOLMES
Puzzle Collection

Dr John Watson

SEVENOAKS

Contents

Introduction 8

ELEMENTARY

STRAIGHTFORWARD

CUNNING

FIENDISH

Introduction

THE NAME OF MY DEAR FRIEND and companion Mr. Sherlock Holmes is familiar to all who possess any interest whatsoever in the field of criminal investigation. Indeed, there are some weeks where it hardly seems possible to pick up a newspaper without seeing his name splashed luridly across the front page. Unlike so many, however, his renown is justly deserved – not for nothing has he frequently been heralded as England's greatest detective, living or dead. Personally, I suspect that his abilities are unmatched anywhere in the world at this time.

I myself have been fortunate enough to share in Holmes' extraordinary adventures, and if I have been unable to rival his insight, I have consoled myself by acting as his de facto chronicler. I also flatter myself a little with the notion that I have, betimes, provided some little warmth of human companionship. We have spent many years, on and off, sharing rooms at 221b Baker Street, and I like to think that the experience has enriched both our existences. My name, though it is of little matter, is John Watson, and I am by profession a doctor.

My dear friend has long had a passionate ambition to improve the minds of humanity. He has often talked about writing a book that will help to instil the habits which he considers so absolutely vital to the art of deduction. Such a tome would be a revolutionary step in the history of mankind, and would most certainly address observation, logical analysis, criminal behaviour, scientific and mathematical knowledge, clear thinking, and much more besides. Alas, it has yet to materialise, for the world is full of villainy, and Sherlock Holmes is ever drawn to the solution of very real problems.

But over the course of our adventures, Holmes has never given up on the cause of improving my modest faculties. On innumerable occasions, he has presented me with opportunities to engage my mind, and solve some problem or other which to him is perfectly clear from the information already available. These trials have sometimes been quite taxing, and have not always come at a welcome moment, but I have engaged in all of them to the very best of my abilities. To do otherwise would be to dishonour the very generous gift my friend is making me in devoting time to my analytical improvement.

In truth, I do believe that his ministrations have indeed helped. I consider myself to be more aware than I was in my youth, and less prone to hasty assessments and faulty conclusions. If I have gained any greater talent in these areas, it is entirely thanks to the efforts that my friend has exerted on my behalf, for it is most certainly not an area for which I am naturally disposed. Give me a sickly patient, and I feel absolutely confident of swiftly arriving at the appropriate diagnosis and, to the limits provided by medical science, of attaining a successful recovery for the poor unfortunate. But my mind does not turn naturally to criminality, violence or deception. If this were a perfect world, then we would all co-exist in genial and honourable honesty, and I would be perfectly suited for the same. Alas, that is far from the case, and my dear friend is far better adapted to the murky undertows of the real world than I.

Still, as I have already attested, Holmes' little trials have had a beneficial effect even on me. For one who is more readily disposed to such efforts, the results may well be commensurately powerful. Thus, I have taken the liberty of assembling this collection.

Working assiduously from my notes, I have compiled somewhere in the region of one hundred and fifty of the puzzles that Holmes has set me over the years. I have been assiduous in ensuring that I have described the situation as I first encountered it, with all pertinent information reproduced. The answers are as detailed as I can usefully make them. Some I managed to answer successfully myself; for others, I have reproduced Holmes' explanations as accurately as my notes permit.

To improve the accessibility a little, I have attempted to order the trials into approximate groupings of difficulty – *elementary*, *straightforward*, *cunning* and *fiendish*, to be exact. Holmes has a devious mind, and there were times when he was entirely determined to baffle me, whilst on other occasions, the problems were simple enough to serve as illustrative examples of certain principles. I believe that I have broadly succeeded in classifying the difficulty of his riddles, but I beg your indulgence in so uncertain a matter. Every question is easy, if you know the answer, and the opposite holds equally true.

If is my fervent hope that you will find this little volume enlightening and amusingly diverting. If it may prove to sharpen your deductive sense a little, that would be all the vindication that I could ever possibly wish; all the credit for such improvement would be due Holmes himself. I, as always, am content to be just the scribe. I have taken every effort to ensure that the problems are all amenable to fair solution, but if by some remote happenchance that should prove not the case, it must be clear that the blame lies entirely on my shoulders, and that none should devolve to my dear companion.

My friends, it is with very real pleasure that I present to you this volume of the puzzles of Mr. Sherlock Holmes.

I remain, as always, your servant,

JHWatson

Dr John H. Watson.

PART ONE

ELEMENTARY

✳

A Matter of Identity

AS WE WERE WALKING THROUGH

Regent's Park one afternoon, on our way to St. John's Wood, Holmes drew my attention to a pair of young women engaged in earnest conversation with a somewhat older man.

"Observe those ladies, Watson. What can you tell me about them?"

I studied them closely. They were as alike as peas in a pod, identical in facial structure, deportment, dress and coiffure. I said as much to my companion, and asserted that they surely had to be twins.

"Indeed?" Holmes looked amused. "For a fact, I can tell you that Louise and Lisa Barnes share the same mother, the same father, and the same precise day of birth, but I'm afraid you are utterly wrong. They are most certainly not twins."

Can you explain?

❋ Solution on page 181 ❋

A Difficult Age

"LOGIC IS PARAMOUNT, WATSON."

Sherlock Holmes was in a thoughtful mood, pacing slowly up and down the length of the sitting room, pipe firmly in hand. "The better able you are to pick apart a problem in your mind and evaluate all of the ramifications it encompasses, the stronger will be your deductive reasoning."

"Of course," I said.

"So, then. Let us say that I know of a particular fellow. Today is a singular occasion, for two days ago, he was 25 years of age, but next year, he will be 28.

How is such a thing possible?"

❋ Solution on page 182 ❋

Cold Feet

"YOU'VE NOTICED, I DARE SAY,

at night, when the flat is cold, that the carpeted floor here in the sitting room feels much warmer than the tiled floor in the bathroom," said Holmes.

"Quite so," I agreed.

"Have you given any thought to why that ought to be the case?"

"Well, the carpet..." I began, trailing off as I realised I had not actually considered the matter.

"But surely you cannot think that the carpet is any different temperature to the tile. The flat is uniformly heated, after all."

"Of course not."

"So why the difference, then?"

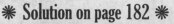

❋ Solution on page 182 ❋

The First Curiosity

HOLMES HAS ON OCCASION EXTOLLED

the virtues of absurdity as a way of breaking free of the confines of regimented thinking. "Watson," he told me once, "the ridiculous is one of the best methods to shatter the iron confines of pedestrian thought."

With that in mind, he engaged in a programme of springing baffling and sometimes ludicrous problems on me at moments when I least expected them.

The first caught me completely unawares.

"I have considered commissioning a house with windows facing south on all four sides," Holmes declared, to my amazement. "Do you think this is a good idea?"

❋ Solution on page 183 ❋

The Fool

INSPECTOR LESTRADE HAD INVEIGLED

Holmes and myself into going with him to Dawes Heath in Essex, where a consignment of goose lard had gone missing under rather peculiar circumstances. We were making our way through the small village when Lestrade suddenly hooted with laughter.

———————◆——————

"You have to see this, Holmes." He beckoned us over to a small, disreputable shack, outside of which a poor wretch was whittling a piece of bark. "This chap is the village idiot," Lestrade said quietly. "He's got not the first clue. Offered the choice between a penny and a shilling, he'll pick the penny every time."

"Is that so?" Holmes sounded amused.

"Watch," said the Inspector. He fished in his pocket for a moment, and then produced the two coins, and offered them grandly to the whittling local. The chap leapt up, and with great noises of appreciation, took the penny and went cavorting off with it, crowing over its coppery sheen. Lestrade looked most pleased with himself.

"If there's a fool here," Holmes said archly, "it's not that fellow."

What did he mean?

✷ **Solution on page 184** ✷

Rabbit Race

"DID YOU EVER ENGAGE IN A RABBIT RACE?"

Holmes' rather peculiar question brought me up short, and I stopped in the street to stare at him. "Why do you ask?"

"I was considering an illustrative question for you, my dear Watson," he said, "such matters can be somewhat revealing."

I shrugged. "Pray continue, if my lack of the requisite experience does not invalidate the problem."

"Not in the least, the problem is quite elementary. Imagine then, if you will, a pair of quite companionable rabbits of long-standing familiarity to each other. Instructed to race for the amusement of children, they are happy enough to amble along at the same speed, keeping each other company and, inevitably, yielding a dead heat."

"That seems plausible enough," I ventured.

"After the race, one of the judges notes that the first half and second half were run in the same time, and that the last quarter lasted as long as the penultimate. If the first three quarters took 6¾ minutes, how long was the entire race?"

✳ Solution on page 184 ✳

The Barrel

"COME WATSON," SAID HOLMES.

"Let's test your mental musculature with a simple challenge."

———————————

"Very well," I replied.

"Imagine you are faced with a sizeable, open-topped barrel of water," Holmes instructed me. "You know that it is close to being half-full, but you do not know whether it is exactly so, or more or less. With no instrument available with which to measure the depth of the water, can you devise a means to ascertain its state?"

✳ Solution on page 185 ✳

The First Mental Trial

"MY DEAR WATSON, A KEEN MIND

must be able to follow a thread of logic through convoluted labyrinths at which even an Ariadne would quail."

"I dare say that's true," said I. "Do I assume that means you have some trial for me?"

"I couldn't say," replied Holmes, "but if you did, that assumption would be well founded."

"Very well," I said. "Pray, go ahead."

"This should prove a gentle warm-up. There is something you own that it is yours, and always has been. Despite this, all your friends use it, whilst you yourself rarely get to make use of it at all. What am I talking about?"

✳ Solution on page 185 ✳

Whistler

"YOU MUST HAVE NOTICED THAT

a kettle gets quieter shortly before it boils," Holmes said.

I nodded agreeably.

"Why is that, would you think?"

✳ Solution on page 186 ✳

The First Literal Oddity

AS YOU MUST BE AWARE, WITH THIS

volume in your hands, I have some very meagre scrapings of ability in the weaving of sentences. I hesitate to call my facility, such as it is, a talent, but I hope I have managed to document my friend's extraordinary adventures in an amusing manner.

In amongst his efforts at improving my very basic skills of deduction and investigation, Holmes from time to time would challenge my linguistic facility. Whilst this was undoubtedly a change of pace from some of his little challenges, he none the less managed to ensure that his wordplay provided me with a genuine test. These trials of his may be diverting to you, and are offered in that spirit.

I was minding my own business one morning, munching on a piece of Mrs. Hudson's toast, when Holmes suddenly barked "Honorificabilitudinitatibus!"

I managed to splutter "I beg your pardon?"

"Honorificabilitudinitatibus, Watson. 'Of honour', more familiarly. You may place some blame for its inclusion in the canon of English at the feet of Master Shakespeare. Or if that monstrosity is not to your taste, how about 'unimaginatively', 'verisimilitudes', or 'parasitological'?"

"I don't follow you," I said.

"What do those words have in common, man? It should be simplicity itself for a fellow of your abilities."

✳ Solution on page 186 ✳

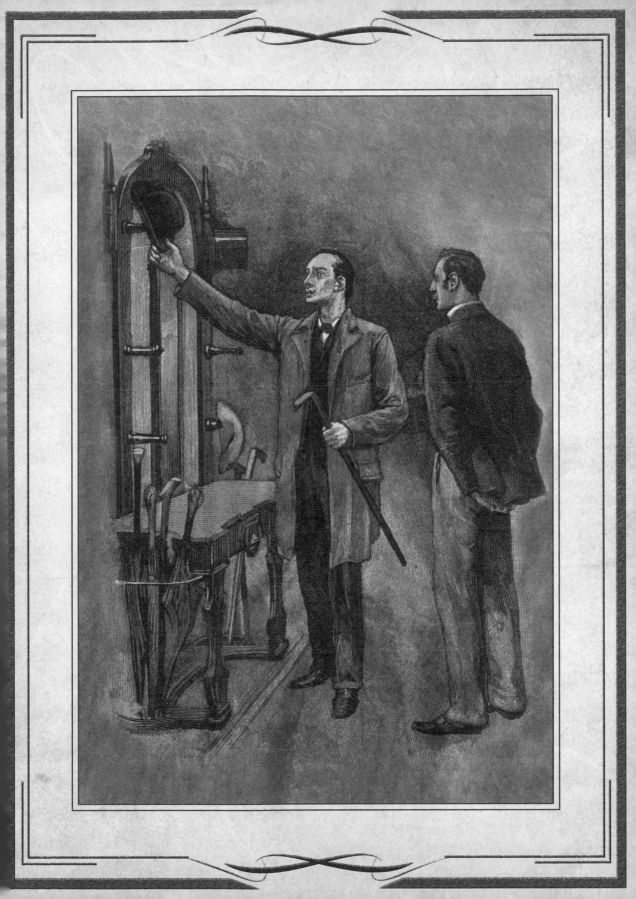

Elementary Geometry

ONE MORNING, AS WE WERE HEADING

into South London, Holmes said to me, "A grasp of elementary geometry is a powerful weapon in the fight against crime."

I admitted that this sounded like sage advice, given the occasional need to apprehend villains by the swiftest route.

"There are other purposes as well," Holmes admonished.

"Of course," I said.

"So here is a basic little matter for you. Assume you are a villain, robbing a warehouse near a straight stretch of the river. Your plan is to carry your goods to the riverside, where a confederate is waiting with a small boat, and then have him sail off casually while you make your way back to a cab, waiting at the entrance to the dock. Obviously you need to make sure that your total route is the shortest possible, as every second may count. How would you go about calculating the precise location of the boat along the river-bank?"

✳ Solution on page 187 ✳

The Meal

THERE WAS ONE OCCASION WHERE I DID

manage to stump the great Sherlock Holmes with a puzzle that vexed him most mightily. The problem is simple. A woman presented a man with some food. He duly ate it. As a direct and absolute consequence of eating it, he died. If he had not eaten it, his death would have been averted.

As I explained in response to Holmes' terse questioning, the food was perfectly pleasant. It was not in the least bit toxic or deleterious, nor did it convey any disease or ailment. It was not stolen, or subject to mistaken identity, and no-one later came looking for it. The man consumed the food successfully, without any discomfort, and with no obstruction of the air passages. In fact, he enjoyed it, and his death was greatly delayed. Never the less, the food he consumed on that specific occasion was solely responsible for his demise.

Can you see the answer that even the world's greatest detective could not?

✷ Solution on page 188 ✷

Eureka

"JOIN ME IN A LITTLE THOUGHT EXERCISE

about fluid dynamics, Watson."

Holmes appeared to be in good humour, and I readily agreed to his suggestion.

"If you place a small boat-like vessel into a tank of water, it will displace a weight of water equal to its own, causing the water level to rise. So it must be clear that if you then put a steel weight inside the vessel, the water level will rise further."

"Indeed."

"So what do you think would happen if you were to throw the weight over the side of the vessel, down into the water? Would the water level rise, remain unchanged, or fall?"

✳ Solution on page 189 ✳

Regent Street

AS WE WERE TRAVELLING ALONG REGENT

Street one evening, Holmes paused to engage a painter who, with his mate, was just finishing up the work of renewing the lamp posts along the street.

Holmes quickly ascertained that the men had been apportioned the east and west sides of the street. One had arrived early, and made a start, but had picked the wrong side. His companion arrived after three posts had been completed, and the chap moved back to start on the correct side. We caught them as they were finishing, and to help speed the process up, the tardier man had switched to his mate's side at the end, and painted six posts for him.

Thus completed, the men were idly curious as to which had painted the more posts, the early fellow or the tardy one, and by how many. They confirmed that there were the same number of posts on both sides

Holmes declared the matter elementary, and indicated I should explain. What would your answer have been?

❊ Solution on page 189 ❊

Rider

"ALLOW ME TO VEX YOU WITH A

little question about a horseback journey," Holmes said to me.

"I am not a comfortable rider these days," I said.

"That is of no matter. It will not affect your appreciation of the question."

I nodded. "Very well."

"On a journey in the country, you travel to your destination at a reasonably sprightly 12 miles per hour. On the return, you set a more modest pace, in deference to your steed's exertions, and manage just 8 miles per hour. What is your average speed for the journey?"

❋ Solution on page 190 ❋

The Second Mental Trial

"I AM GOING OUT FOR A WHILE, WATSON."

"I trust you will have a congenial time," I replied.

"I feel it can be made more profitable by the combination of a little business with a little mental work on your part," Holmes told me.

"Oh?"

"I will cheerfully buy you a cup of tea if you meet me on the corner of the Strand at a precise time."

"And when is that?"

"That should be an elementary matter for you to deduce, my friend. Three hours before the meeting time is as long after three in the morning as it is in advance of three in the afternoon. Will I see you there?"

I assured him that he would. Could you have done the same?

❋ Solution on page 191 ❋

The Gang

ONE EVENING, AFTER SHERLOCK

Holmes and myself had provided some assistance to Scotland Yard on a matter of some delicacy, Inspector Lestrade took the opportunity to challenge my companion with what he hoped would prove a vexatious riddle. His hopes were unfounded of course, but I'm sure that comes as no surprise.

"I was at a break-in yesterday, Mr. Holmes," began the Inspector. "Nasty business. A group of burly young men apprehended a man and his wife outside their home, and forcibly restrained them there. Meanwhile, two of their number kicked the door straight off its hinges and charged in there. They came out a few minutes later with the couple's most precious treasure. Then, to top it all off, rather than scarpering like your usual villain would, they handed their loot over to the weeping wife, and went about their business. I saw the whole thing, but I didn't make even a single arrest. What do you make of that?"

❋ Solution on page 191 ❋

The Hampstead Twins

WE RETURNED TO 221B BAKER STREET

late one evening, after having spent the day chasing around Blackheath. Mrs Hudson was kind enough to bring us a very welcome pot of tea, and a plate of biscuits. Before leaving, she looked across at Holmes and myself.

"Have I ever told you fine gents about my niece Katie?"

I shook my head, but Holmes recalled that she was a maid for a couple somewhere up in Hampstead.

"That's her," said Mrs. Hudson. "She was telling me last week that the youngsters of the family had just been celebrating their birthdays. Twins, they are, a boy and a girl. Born within fifteen minutes of each other. But the younger one's birthday came two clear days before the elder's. Can you make sense of it?"

❋ Solution on page 192 ❋

The First Portmanteau

"OBSERVATION, ANALYSIS, DEDUCTION."

Holmes punctuated each word with a brisk rap on the arm of his chair. "These are the cornerstones of the art of investigation. I want you to study this little arrangement I've had drawn, Watson."

I agreed to do so of course, but confessed a certain bemusement as to what I was looking for. I have copied it for you, of course.

"It is a visual portmanteau, old chap. The image contains a number of clues referring to a rather well-known spot in London. Different elements of the picture show different aspects of the location, and in combination, there is only one place on Earth where it could possibly be. You should be able to identify it rather easily, I think."

I looked again, and you know, Holmes was right. There was only one place the image could refer to. Do you know where?

✳ Solution on page 193 ✳

The Third Mental Trial

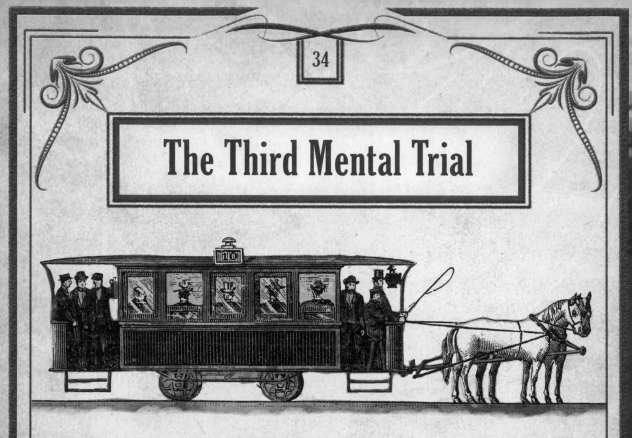

"MY DEAR WATSON, WILL YOU UNDERSTAND

my meaning when I inform you that an entirely hypothetical acquaintance of mine, Alfie, told me about a bus journey he had recently made."

"I see," I said. "This is by way of a puzzle."

"Quite so. Alfie told me that his bus was quite busy, and he was initially unable to seat himself. His fortunes changed at the half-way mark however, and he finally got the chance to take the weight off his feet. When he had just one half as far to go again to his destination as the distance for which he had been seated, an infirm gentleman boarded the bus, and Alfie generously gave up his place for the man. At the end of his journey, he decided to calculate the proportion for which he had managed to avoid standing. Can you tell me what it was?"

✳ Solution on page 194 ✳

Catford

"I HEARD OF A SCHOOLMISTRESS,

**down in Catford, with a rather peculiar morning ceremonial,"
Holmes told me.**

"The mind boggles," I replied. Catford can be a queer place, although it is rightly famed for its historic curry house.

"It is her habit," he continued, "to start the school day with a series of polite bows. Each boy must bow to each other boy, and then to each girl, and then to the teacher. Likewise, each girl must bow to each other girl, and then to each boy, and then to the teacher. The whole process requires 900 obeisances. If I tell you that there are twice as many girls in the school as boys, you will undoubtedly be able to tell me how many boys there are there."

"Undoubtedly," I replied drily.

Can you solve the issue?

❊ Solution on page 194 ❊

The Second Curiosity

I WAS READING SOME PATIENT NOTES

one evening. I was quite absorbed, so when Holmes said, "I believe there to be a place that is located between England and France, yet is further from England than France actually is."

———————

"Great heavens!" I exclaimed, startled out of my contemplation.

"Not quite," Holmes remarked wryly. "Care to make a more terrestrial guess?"

❋ Solution on page 195 ❋

Trains

"YOU KNOW HOW IMPORTANT IT CAN BE

to have a clear impression of the way that trains perform in this day and age, Watson. Entire cases can hang on it."

―――――◆―――――

I agreed whole-heartedly.

"A sense of timing in these matters is highly desirable. So pray, consider this little matter. Two trains start on a journey at the same moment, each headed to the origin point of the other, via parallel tracks. When they pass each other, the slower still has four hours to travel to its destination, whilst the faster has just one hour still to go. How many times faster is the one going than the other?"

✻ Solution on page 196 ✻

Oval

"IF I GAVE YOU A PAIR OF COMPASSES,"

Holmes said to me, "You would of course know how to construct a circle."

———— ◆ ◆ ◆ ————

"Of course," I said, feelingly slightly put out that such a basic matter would even be mentioned.

"I mean no slight, my dear Watson. However, I do wonder if you would know how to construct an oval with just one sweep of the pencil?"

✳ Solution on page 197 ✳

Gloucester

WE WERE INVESTIGATING A MATTER

concerning a Gloucester cattle-man, a nasty storm, and some peculiar stone shards. One of the elements of the case involved the degree to which the fellow was watering his 'honest' milk.

A maid, tired of her employer, was able to inform us of the procedure. He started with two kegs, one – the smaller – of milk, and the other of water.

He then manipulated the milk as follows. First, he poured enough water into the smaller keg to double the contents. Then he poured back enough of the mix into the larger keg to in turn double its contents. Finally, he poured liquid from the larger keg into the smaller until both held the same volume.

Then he sent the larger keg to London, as the finished product. Can you say what amount of the final blend was actually milk?

✳ Solution on page 197 ✳

Wiggins

ON ONE MEMORABLE MORNING,

young Wiggins, the lead scamp of Holmes' Baker Street Irregulars, put a poser to me after completing some small errand for his master. It is my suspicion that secretly he wanted to put the question to Holmes himself, but either lacked the nerve, or feared that it would be too trivial a matter for the great man.

If the latter, then he made his choice wisely.

"Here guv'nor," Wiggins said to me, "I've got a little riddle. What do you say we wager a farthing on your being able to solve it."

"Is that so? A farthing. Very well. What will you give me if I have the answer?"

"A smile," said the little rascal. "Surely you wouldn't take money from one such as myself, Doctor."

"Very well," I said. "I enjoy a challenge."

"You won't regret it, sir. So, tell me, what occurs once in June, once in July, and twice in August?"

My first thought was the full moon, but I quickly discarded that as not being the case in this year. "Hmm," I said. I could see Holmes' eyes glittering with amusement, but he said nothing, and left the matter to me to resolve.

✸ Solution on page 198 ✸

To Catch a Thief

ONE NIGHT IN DEPTFORD, WE WERE

waiting in a house for a burglar to attend. The man appeared as expected, but managed to turn heel and flee. Holmes shot after him as swiftly as possible.

———————

He returned after a short space, with the burglar in tow. I enquired as to how difficult it had proven to catch the fellow.

"It was a simple matter," Holmes replied. "By the time I left the house, he had a 27-step lead, and he was taking eight steps to my five. It would have been bleak, save for the fact that he is a short man, and two of my strides were worth five of his. In fact, from that, you should be able to tell me how many strides I required to apprehend the scoundrel."

✳ Solution on page 198 ✳

The Second Literal Oddity

I WAS READING QUIETLY ONE EVENING

in Baker Street when Holmes put down his violin and turned to me.

"I have another little lexical trial for you, if you are of a mind to accept," said he.

"Of course," I replied.

"Capital. Ponder then upon the words 'cabbaged' and 'fabaceae', the latter being of leguminous fame. What oddness do they share, and why might I remark upon it?"

✳ Solution on page 199 ✳

Cheapside

WE WERE ENGAGED ON SOME BUSINESS

on Cheapside one afternoon when Holmes turned to me.

———◆———

"Answer me something, Watson," he said.

"Of course," I replied.

"If there is a fellow whose mother is my mother's mother-in-law, then who is he to me?"

It occurred to me that Holmes must have been talking to Mrs. Hudson again. I put this to him, and he did not deny it, but required an answer none the less. Can you reckon it out?

✷ Solution on page 200 ✷

The Third Curiosity

"QUICK, WATSON!" HOLMES PASSED ME A

small pad and a pencil. "Write down the numeric figures for twelve thousand, twelve hundred and twelve pounds!"

I paused, momentarily confounded. "What?"

✳ Solution on page 200 ✳

Walker

SHORTLY BEFORE THE TRAGIC MURDER

of the Clapham trapeze artist, I had been watching another aerial acrobat performing a daring routine on a high wire. Armed with only a long, saggy bar, he practically danced back and forth across the hall from his lofty position.

"Daring fellow," I remarked to Holmes as he finished his routine.

"Less so than you might think," replied Holmes cryptically.

Any idea what he meant?

✳ Solution on page 201 ✳

Swinging Pendulums

"I HAVE A LITTLE PHYSICAL SCIENCE
question in mind for you, Watson."

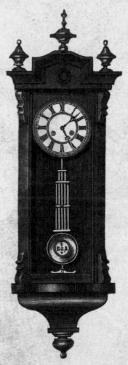

I nodded. "I'll do my best," I said.

"Imagine a vacuum jar with a pair of pendulums suspended inside. They are identical, the same size bob, of the same material, at the end of the same length of string. Set them swinging together – with a careful shake, perhaps – and they will move identically, as you would expect."

"Indeed," I said, "I'm glad to hear it, for I would have been stymied were it not the case."

"Now, if you let out the string slightly on one of them, it will slow that bob down, so that the elongated one falls behind the swing of the other."

"Very well," I said.

"What do you think would happen if instead of lengthening the string, I changed one of the bobs for a substantially lighter material?"

✳ Solution on page 202 ✳

Rice

HOLMES AND I HAD SAT DOWN

to a light supper of bread and soup. I asked him to pass the salt cellar, which was a little out of the way, and he picked it up to hand to me. Then he paused, thoughtfully.

———◆———

"You know, my dear Watson, we should add a little rice to this cellar."

"Rice? Whatever for?"

He looked at me. "Can you not work it out?"

❊ Solution on page 203 ❊

The Board

HOLMES INFORMED ME THAT THE

senior management of one of the larger London banks had suffered something of a split over a matter of a slightly risky investment policy. Despite a group meeting to attempt some sort of arbitration over the debate, the situation became heated, and a substantial chunk of the attendees marched out in high dudgeon.

"If the chairman had gone with the rebels," Holmes noted, "A full two thirds of the meeting would have left. But on the other hand, had he been able to persuade his putative allies, his deputy and the financial officer, to remain, the departees would have made up just one half of the group."

"I see," I said.

"Quite so," he replied. "Can you then tell me how many men were at the meeting?"

❋ Solution on page 203 ❋

An Issue of Age

HOLMES AND I WERE TAKING LUNCHEON

when he offered me a test of my ingenuity to season the meal. I accepted, and he posited the following rather remarkable case.

"Let us say that there is a married couple. The wife is younger than the husband, and it so happens that her age is equal to the digits of his age reversed. Given that the difference in their ages is equal to exactly an eleventh of their sum, can you tell me how old the lady is?"

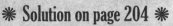

✳ Solution on page 204 ✳

Almonds

AFTER ONE PARTICULARLY SUCCESSFUL

mission on the part of the Baker Street Irregulars, in addition to paying the three boys involved the agreed-upon bonus, he also gave them a very large bag of sugared almonds, boasting 840 sweets in total.

The boys decided to share the sweets exactly on the basis of their ages, which totalled 28. For every seven sweets that the eldest took, the one in the middle took six; for every four that the one in the middle claimed, the youngest got three.

Can you tell how old the boys were?

❋ Solution on page 205 ❋

The Fontaignes

"DO YOU KNOW OF LORD AND
Lady Fontaigne, Watson?"

They were minor luminaries on the social scene, and I said as much.

"It is their wedding anniversary today."

"How delightful for them," I replied.

"Possibly," Holmes mused. "Did you know that nineteen years ago, when they married, Lady Fontaigne was just one third of her husband's age. Today, he is but twice as old as she is."

"Remarkable."

"Quite. Can you deduce how old Lady Fontaigne was on her wedding day?"

❋ Solution on page 205 ❋

PART TWO

STRAIGHTFORWARD

✳ ✳

The Signpost

I WAS CLEANING MY PIPE WHEN MY

dear friend intruded upon my reverie with what he described as a little test of my ingenuity.

———— ◆ ————

"Imagine that we are out in the wilds of the countryside following a clue towards the solution of some horrid crime, Watson. It should be easy enough to do. Somewhere reasonably unfamiliar to you. Derbyshire, say."

"Very well," I said. "Derbyshire."

"We departed the hamlet of Mercaston at the same time, and made our separate ways into Ravensdale Park. We are to meet in the village of Mugginton, once I've had a look at the 'Halter Devil' chapel. You know that the local paths will guide you between the two, but otherwise you are utterly unclear as to where Mugginton actually lies."

"That takes little imagination," I muttered.

"You are walking along the path when you come to a five-fold junction. There is a signpost which shows which village lies along which path, but to your dismay it has been blown over, and you have no idea which of your four options might carry you to Mugginton. Could you find your way?"

❊ Solution on page 207 ❊

Water into Wine

"HERE IS A LITTLE QUESTION

for you, Watson." I indicated my readiness to engage my brain.

"I take two wine glasses, one twice the size of the other. I fill the smaller half-way, and the larger just to one third. Then I fill the remaining space in both glasses with water."

"I'm glad this is a theoretical issue," I noted.

"If I then pour both glasses into a previously empty pitcher," Holmes continued, "can you tell me what proportion of the resulting liquid is wine?"

✳ Solution on page 208 ✳

Alby

"IT'S LIKE THIS, MR. HOLMES,"

said the redoubtable Mrs. Hudson one morning.

"My cousin Alby works at the Millwall Iron Works. He's a supervisor, as it happens. Every morning at 8 o'clock sharp, he makes his way down the stairs. When he gets to his destination a little afterwards, he brews himself a cup of tea, and then settles down with the morning papers. There's a boy who sells them just on the corner by the main gate of the works. I know for a fact that he hardly manages to get half-way through the paper before he's sound asleep, and he remains flat out for the next eight hours. Judgement Day itself would have a hard timing waking our Alby. Yet even so, management are very happy with his performance and the amount of work he puts in. How do you think that can be?"

✳ Solution on page 209 ✳

The Third Literal Oddity

"CONSIDER THE HUMBLE GOATGRASS,

Watson." Holmes was pacing back and forth in a thoughtful manner, and these were his first words for some time. I looked at him curiously.

"Aegilops is the genus. Bears a striking similarity to winter wheat. Or if Aegilops isn't to your fancy, then how about 'billowy', or 'ghosty'? For that matter, let us not forget 'spoonfeed'."

The penny dropped. "One of your word-plays."

"English is a marvellously eccentric language," Holmes said, by way of agreement.

What is curious about the words he mentioned?

❋ Solution on page 210 ❋

The Time

HOLMES AND MYSELF WERE MAKING

our way back to Baker Street after a disappointingly fruitless day when a fellow across the street hailed us somewhat abruptly.

"You! I say, you, in the odd hat! Tell me the time!"

Holmes looked over at him. "If you add a quarter of the time from midday up to now to half the time remaining from now to midday on the morrow, you will have the precisely correct time."

"I say," the man said, more quietly, and walked on.

Do you know what time it was?

❋ Solution on page 211 ❋

The Fourth Curiosity

I WAS ENGAGED IN THE PERUSAL

of an entertaining volume when Holmes startled me somewhat by suddenly pushing my book down.

"Tell me, my dear Watson. By what part does four fourths exceed three fourths?"

"A fourth," I replied irritably.

Holmes looked at me quizzically. "Really?"

❋ Solution on page 211 ❋

A Very Hudson Christmas

MRS HUDSON BROUGHT ANOTHER MATTER

of her confusing relations to Holmes and myself one December evening, more out of a desire to provide us with a little vexatious entertainment I think than out of any genuine uncertainty on her part.

"Gentlemen," she said, "I am hosting a gathering of some of my family this year. In addition to myself, I shall be entertaining two grandparents, four parents, one father-in-law, one mother-in-law, one brother, two sisters, four children, two sons, two daughters, three grandchildren, and not least, one daughter-in-law. Fortunately, there are no brothers-in-law to deal with. I'm curious as to how many places I need set."

"You'll need a mighty table, Mrs Hudson," said I.

"Not necessarily," Holmes declared.

What is the least number of people that may be involved?

✷ Solution on page 212 ✷

Drifts

ONE SNOWY MORNING IN JANUARY,

Holmes paused in the street to bring a curious fact to my attention. Strong winds had driven the snow into drifts along the side of the pavement, but as he pointed out, there was a proportionately far greater deposit of snow against the side of the nearby telegraph pole than there was against the side of the house which lay some dozen or so yards beyond it.

It would have seemed to me that the opposite really ought to have been the case, but after a little thought I was able to demonstrate to Holmes that I could fathom the answer to his satisfaction. What was it?

✷ Solution on page 212 ✷

Davy

HOLMES PUT HIS PAPER DOWN

and looked over at me one morning. "You've seen a Davy Lamp, I assume?"

"Those things miners use to prevent explosions, I believe. Basically an oil lamp surrounded by a fine wire mesh."

"That's the one," Holmes said. "They're popular because they won't cause an explosion when brought into contact with firedamp. The ill-educated sometimes believe that the reason for this is that the mesh is too fine for the gas to get through, which is of course nonsense. But can you divine the actual reason?"

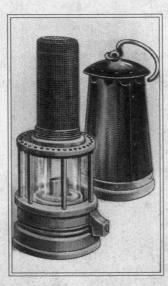

❋ Solution on page 213 ❋

The Fourth Mental Trial

"I WAS TALKING TO MY HYPOTHETICAL

acquaintance Alfie earlier," Holmes said.

I declared that this statement appeared to herald another mental test.

"Indeed. I enquired as to Alfie's age. He, in turn, informed me that in six years time, he would be one and a quarter times the age that he was four years ago."

"I suppose you want me to tell you his age."

"Please do," said Holmes.

✳ Solution on page 214 ✳

Suffolk

"I WANT YOU TO GIVE SOME THOUGHT
to three villages in Suffolk, Watson."

I was getting used to Holmes' trials by this point. "Real ones?"

"Real enough, although I am taking flagrant liberties with their actual geography. Consider Crowfield, Hemingstone and Gosbeck."

"They have suitably resonant names."

"Quite. So. Let us say that Hemingstone is directly south of Crowfield, and is connected by a straight road. Gosbeck is off to the east, some 12 miles as the raven flies from the Hemingstone-Crowfield road, and closer to Hemingstone than it is to Crowfield. It is your intention to travel from Hemingstone to Crowfield, but by a slight mishap, you discover that you have instead taken the route via Gosbeck. The roads are equally straight. On arriving at your destination, you discover that the route you used is 35 miles long. How many extra miles did your route take you?"

✳ Solution on page 214 ✳

The Fire

"AH, HERE'S A DIVERTING LITTLE

question for you, Watson."

"You are trapped in a small, unkempt valley. It is just a few hundred yards in length, less than that in width, and surrounded almost entirely by stern cliffs that defeat your ability to climb. Some blackguard, who means you ill, has lit a fire at the far end, and the prevailing wind is blowing it straight up the valley towards you. Shelter is not an option. There is no source of water. You have only your usual accoutrements -- pocket watch, pistol, notepad, pencil, pipe, tobacco and matches. Can you formulate a plan that will prevent you from being roasted alive?"

✳ Solution on page 215 ✳

The Will

HOLMES' ASSISTANCE WAS SOUGHT

in arbitrating a rather difficult bequest. He did so in customary fashion, with just an idle word or two, but it was to the petitioner's satisfaction.

The will was made by a man whose wife was pregnant. He knew he would not live to see the child's arrival, and so dictated that that if the child was a boy, he should get two thirds of the estate, and the wife one third. If, on the other hand, the child was a girl, the wife was to get two thirds, and the daughter one third. How one ranks these matters so clinically is beyond me, but that is not the issue here.

However, after he had died, his wife gave birth to twins, one male and one female. The question put to Holmes was regarding how to settle the estate in accordance with the wishes of the deceased.

Can you see a way?

✳ Solution on page 215 ✳

Modesty

"I WAS FACED WITH A MODEST

young lady the other day," Holmes said to me. "She was
chary of confessing her true age."

—————— ◆ ——————

"As many women are," I noted.

"Quite so. I was reasonably persuasive on the matter however,
and finally got her to admit that she was the eldest of fifteen
children, each born with a year and a half between them.
When she confessed that her age was eight times that of the
youngest of her siblings, I knew at once how old she was."

How old was she?

❋ Solution on page 216 ❋

The House

ON ONE OCCASION WHICH YOU MAY RECALL

if you have seen some of my other notes, Sherlock Holmes and I encountered a young woman with a most peculiar problem. She had been picked over scores of other candidates for a position as a nanny just outside Winchester. The one immutable requirement was that she cut her hair to a particular style. She was paid at an exorbitantly generous rate, and given the most eccentric duties.

Her housework was far lighter than any girl would have suspected. Indeed, she was completely barred from one of the areas of the house. So her domestic work was light at best. On top of that, the child of the family was of an age where he barely seemed to need much supervision. In fact, he clearly resented the intrusion. There were times however when she was required to don particular outfits of clothes, sit in precise locations within the house, and engage in various social pursuits. At these times, the father and mother of the house were sociable and jolly. Outside of these times, they were far less engaged.

As if that was not enough to deal with, the house also had a persistent observer, a small fellow who seemed to hang about watching intently at all sorts of queer hours. Strange noises were heard inside the building from time to time as well. The young woman grew increasingly disturbed with the oddness of her situation, and turned to Holmes for an explanation. He was able to provide one almost immediately.

Can you?

✳ Solution on page 216 ✳

The Beachcomber

"LOOK HERE, WATSON." HOLMES WAS

standing by the window of our flat in Baker Street. I went over to him, and looked where he was pointing. "This is a rare chance to see a distinctive fellow indeed – an estuary beachcomber."

I looked carefully, and saw that Holmes was indicating a raggedly dressed fellow with rather wild looking hair.

"Look at the deep tan of his face," Holmes urged. "Have you ever seen such a burnt hue?" I had not, and said as much. "No other vocation burns the skin quite so. Have you any idea why that might be?"

✳ Solution on page 217 ✳

The Seventh Sword

A PRICELESS SWORD WITH ASSOCIATIONS

to Mary, Queen of Scots had been stolen from an estate, and Holmes had agreed to lend his services in the matter. The local constabulary was making much of the thief's escape, and sought to ascertain which of the nearby villages was the closest – Shenstone, Rushock or Chaddesley.

The sword's custodian expressed his opinion that it seemed as if all three were as far away as each other, although he had never actually attempted to measure the distances involved. The sergeant maintained that the exact distance was important to know.

It was known that the distance from Shenstone to Chaddesley was one and a half miles, from Shenstone to Rushock was one and three tenths miles, and from Rushock to Chaddesley was one and two fifths miles.

Can you discern the distance from the estate to the villages?

✳ Solution on page 218 ✳

The Wood Merchant

LATE LAST AUGUST, A CURIOUS LITTLE

incident occurred in Torquay, and an innocent man very nearly found himself the unfortunate victim of a miscarriage of justice. Over the course of one weekend, three local businesses were burgled of a substantial sum of valuables. A number of witnesses reported catching glimpses of a suspicious figure -- a distinctive looking man, tall, muscular and well tanned, with a prominent nose and a great big bushy beard.

Local police suspected that the beard was a disguise, and after some diligent searching, they located a straight razor and a mound of facial hair in a quiet nook not far from the rear of one of the burglary sites. Suspicion fell on a local wood merchant, who was undeniably tall, tanned, muscular, clean-shaven and nasally endowed; furthermore, the fellow made deliveries of firewood to all three of the businesses. He had been out of the town over that weekend, and therefore had no plausible alibi.

It was the man himself who made contact with Holmes, laying out the above details and begging for aid in clearing his name. Holmes didn't feel any need to take the case on, but he did send the chap a brief note pointing out one salient fact. This alone was sufficient for the fellow to persuade the police to discount him entirely, as his effusive letter of thanks later attested.

Can you think what Holmes told the chap?

✷ Solution on page 219 ✷

The Dark Marriage

HOLMES WAVED HIS NEWSPAPER

at me one morning. "There is a curious tangle in the announcements today, my friend."

"Is that so?" I asked.

"We have here the announcement of a recently deceased fellow who, so it says, married the sister of his widow."

"What the devil? He married his widow's sister?"

"Quite so," Holmes replied. "It appears to be perfectly accurate."

How is it possible, given that it is not possible for the dead to marry?

❊ Solution on page 219 ❊

The Fourth Literal Oddity

"TIME TO EXERCISE YOUR WRITERLY MIND

again, my friend. Turn your thoughts to the words 'scraunched' and 'strengthed'. The former means 'to have made a crunching noise', as if one had walked on gravel; the latter is long out of use, but means, as might be surmised, 'to summon ones strength'. Whilst you are contemplating these singular words, you may also like to think on their counterpart 'Io'. She was a legendary priestess, one of Zeus' many ill-fated conquests in the Greek mythologies."

I confess that I did not reply to Holmes, having been already distracted by the challenge. What do you make of it?

✳ Solution on page 220 ✳

Port and Brandy

"ANSWER ME THIS," HOLMES SAID TO ME

one evening, as we were relaxing after dinner. "The decanter of port and the decanter of brandy over there are both around half full. Let us assume, for the sake of convenience, that they contain identical measures of liquid. Now, imagine I were to pour off a shot of port, and exactly decant it into the brandy jar. I then follow this action by shaking the brandy to mix the blend, and pour off a second shot, of the mix this time. I finish up by tipping the mixed shot back into the port."

———◆———

"Sounds like a devilish mess," I said.

"Actually, an even blend of the two is quite remarkably potable. But that is by the by. Do you suppose there is now more port in the brandy, or more brandy in the port?"

❋ Solution on page 220 ❋

The Fifth Mental Trial

"I WAS WITH WIGGINS EARLIER,"

Holmes told me. "He and a couple of the other irregulars had it in mind to buy a rather attractive ball to play knock-about with. The trouble was that the thing cost 18 pence, and they had only 15 pence between them, all in farthings. They asked for a little assistance. I informed them that if they had sixty farthings between themselves, I had exactly three coins less in my pocket than the average number of coins possessed by the four of us. If they could tell me how many coins I had, I'd pass them a thruppenny bit."

"Did they manage it?"

"Oh yes, Wiggins is a sharp little scamp. Could you have done the same?"

❋ Solution on page 221 ❋

Squares

"I HAVE ANOTHER MATHEMATICAL

conundrum for you," Holmes told me, provoking an entirely involuntary little shudder.

I managed to keep my face from displaying any distress, however.

Holmes, being Holmes of course, had noticed my discomfort anyway. "Fear not," he said. "I'm confident that it is well within your powers. I'd like you to arrange the nine digits in such a way as to have them form four separate numbers, each one perfectly square. Each number from 1 to 9 should be used exactly once, nothing more."

1 3 7 2 8 4 9 5 6

✳ Solution on page 222 ✳

Stamina

DURING MY MILITARY TRAINING IN INDIA,

we were frequently sent on punishing missions to build up our stamina for when we saw actual service in Afghanistan. Those were challenging times, but the sense of accomplishment from getting through the various trials really drove one to excel. As you might imagine, our instructors encouraged us to our best efforts through a system of minor rewards and other inducements.

One particular afternoon still stands out in my memory. We had been sent on a twenty-mile hike through the variable local terrain, leaving shortly before the scorching local noon, with no supplies save a half-pint canteen of water. Our instructions were to make our way round a specific route without stopping for rest or forage; the first man back would win himself lighter duties for the following day. I was stronger then, and put in what I thought was a good showing. By the end of the course, I was as thirsty as a bull, staggering from the heat, caked in dust and grime.

As I arrived, I saw that at least one other chap had narrowly beaten me in. He was in a dreadful state, collapsed on the ground panting, drenched in sweat. Our sergeant was clearly waiting for him to catch his breath. He gave him a few moments, and then proceeded to roundly curse the fellow for a shirker and a cheat, and assigned him to latrine work for the next three days. Then he turned to me, and despite my sudden concerns, told me I was the fourth in, and to go refresh myself.

Holmes understood the sergeant's reaction immediately, of course. Do you?

✳ Solution on page 222 ✳

The Fifth Curiosity

"I'VE HAD WORD," HOLMES TOLD ME

over breakfast, "of a fellow who has turned up some curious coins in his allotment."

"Fortunate for him."

"I dare say," Holmes replied. "He reports that one of the coins is dated as far back as 51 B.C., while another is clearly marked 'Henry I'. What do you make of it?"

✳ Solution on page 223 ✳

The Second Portmanteau

"WATSON, ARE YOU IN THE MOOD FOR
something of a challenge?"

Holmes seemed in high spirits, and was clutching a document of some sort. I allowed that I was game for whatever he happened to have in mind.

"Capital," Holmes said. "You will recall the portmanteau image I brought to your attention some time ago, of course."

"Indeed," I replied. "A composite picture in which each element was a clue to the identity of a certain spot within London."

"Quite. I have another for you, almost as straightforward as the last. In the spirit of fairness however, I must confess that the location is actually slightly outside of London, on this occasion."

So saying, he handed me the sheet of paper he bore. I have duplicated it for your attention. Can you deduce where it points to?

✳ Solution on page 224 ✳

Forty-Eight

"THE NUMBER 48 IS SOMEWHAT CURIOUS,"
Holmes said to me.

"Really?" I mulled it over. "It has never seemed particularly special to me."

"Ah," said Holmes, "but if you add 1 to it, you get a square number – 49, clearly – and if you halve it, and then add 1 to the half, you get another square number, 25. There are a multitude of such numbers of course, but 48 is the smallest. Do you think you can find the next larger one?

✳ Solution on page 226 ✳

The Shoreditch Bank Job

"I HAVE A LITTLE PUZZLE THAT OUGHT TO
appeal to you, Watson."

I allowed that it was a distinct possibility, and encouraged Sherlock Holmes to go ahead.

"A couple of fellows who are... familiar to me were, last month, discussing the best way to break into a particular bank in Shoreditch. I know for a fact that they even enticed a local constable into entering their discussions, and clearing up some of their uncertainties for them. He was fully aware of what they were about; the bank, of course, had absolutely no idea, and so far as I know, still has no clue regarding their identities. Last week their plans bore fruit, and brought them a substantial sum of money. They duly gave a modest percentage of it to the constable who had been so helpful."

"My word! Have you informed the authorities?"

"I have not, my friend. None of the conspirators has done anything the least bit wrong."

Can you deduce what Holmes was talking about?

※ Solution on page 226 ※

The Day of the Book

IT WAS APRIL 23ʳᵈ, AND I WAS GAZING

idly out of the window of 221b at the preponderance of St. George's Cross flags which had appeared in celebration of our patron.

"He was from Palestine, you know." Holmes had followed my gaze, and my train of thought.

"Indeed," I said.

"He is much beloved in Catalonia too -- where it is traditional to give a book, and a rose. An interesting feature, given that it is also the anniversary of the deaths of both Shakespeare and Cervantes. In fact, they died in the same year too, 1616. It would have been a bleak day for literature... if they had not passed away more than a week apart, that is."

Can you explain this odd statement?

✴ Solution on page 227 ✴

The Cross of St. George

"WHILE WE ARE CONSIDERING

St. George," Holmes said, "I have a little matter for you to wrestle with concerning his flag."

———————————

"Oh, really?"

"In shape a centrally placed and evenly sized cross of red against a white field, it is possible -- desirable, even -- to so balance the size of the cross so that the red fabric occupies exactly the same area of the flag as the white fabric. Let us suggest a flag that is four feet wide and three feet high. How wide should the arm of the cross be?"

✳ Solution on page 228 ✳

The Somewhat Crooked Butler

"CONSIDER A SOMEWHAT CROOKED
butler, Watson.".

I found that image to fit well within my experience, and said so.

"Quite so. This fellow has been drawing off his master's ale. Let us say he fills a generous jug from a ten-gallon keg, and replaces the missing volume with water. Some time later, he repeats the exact procedure. After he has done so, he discovers that the keg now contains a blend of exactly half ale and half water, not unlike that in some pubs of my acquaintance. How large is his jug?"

❋ Solution on page 228 ❋

Campanology

CHURCH BELLS ARE A FAMILIAR SOUND

on any London Sunday, often coming from an impressive diversity of directions. I was listening to the soothing peals of one of the churches one morning when Holmes approached me with one of his challenges.

"As a little idle diversion," he said to me, "can you construct a peal for three bells that rings each possible combination once and once alone. Between any two changes, a bell may move just one position in the order, and the cycle must end in such a place that it can repeat without breaking this condition. Furthermore, no bell may be rung either first or last in more that two successive changes."

I must have looked a little daunted, for he added "Fear not, my dear Watson, it is not a trying exercise. Four bells would be a sterner task."

Can you solve the problem?

✸ Solution on page 229 ✸

C

ONE MORNING, HOLMES HANDED ME THE

following enigmatic message on a piece of paper:

1 2 3 4 5 6 7 8 9 = 100

I looked it over, and asked if it were perhaps some sort of code.

"Not in the least, my dear Watson," came the reply. "It is a mathematical riddle for you. There are several ways to add mathematical operators to this list of numbers to ensure that the statement becomes mathematically accurate. The easiest, for example, is to turn the line into 1+2+3+4+5+6+7+ (8x9). That solution requires nine separate mathematical operators however -- one multiplication sign, seven addition signs, and one pair of brackets."

"I see," I managed.

"Permitting yourself just the previously mentioned operators and, additionally, the minus sign and the division sign, what is the least number of operators you can use that still has the sum make sense? You cannot move numbers around at all, but you may combine adjacent numbers into a single value, so that 1 and 2 become 12; this does not cost you an operator."

Can you find the answer?

✹ Solution on page 230 ✹

The Hudson Clan

"CAN YOU SORT OUT A LITTLE MATTER

of kinship for me, Mr. Holmes?" Mrs. Hudson had just brought up the morning's post.

Holmes looked up at her with a distracted glance. "I dare say so, Mrs Hudson. What appears to be the problem."

"Well," she said, "I've been trying to figure it out. If Sally Shaw is my third cousin once removed, on my mother's side -- which she is -- then what relation is her grandmother to my son?"

A knotty problem. Can you find an answer?

✳ Solution on page 231 ✳

Cousin Jennifer

ONE EVENING RECENTLY, AFTER OUR

housekeeper Mrs. Hudson had brought us a pot of tea, she turned to Sherlock Holmes with an uncharacteristically mischievous smile. "I have a little poser that I fancy might amuse you for a moment or two, Mr. Holmes, if you care to hear it."

Sherlock arched an eyebrow. "Go ahead, by all means."

"Well then Mr. Holmes, the long and the short of it is that my cousin Jennifer just got out of London Hospital on Whitechapel Road. She'd been there for a week, and her with nothing wrong with herself whatsoever. No illness, no injury, no mental problems, nothing. Not a word of complaint from her, before, during or after. But they kept her in for a whole week, and wouldn't let her do a single thing for herself. Why, they wouldn't even let her touch a knife or a fork. And to cap it all off, when they finally let her go, she had to be carried bodily from the place. What do you make of that?"

Holmes smiled thinly. "It's clear enough, Mrs. Hudson. What say you, Watson?"

✳ Solution on page 231 ✳

The Fifth Literal Oddity

HOLMES' NEXT LITTLE LINGUISTIC

challenge came after dinner one restful evening. He had just solved a rather hair-raising case involving a murdered seaman, and we were making the most of a very welcome moment of peace and quiet.

"I have a pair of words for you, old friend," Holmes said.

"Pray, go ahead," I replied.

"They are 'facetiously' and 'abstemiously'. In addition, I'll also offer you the word 'subcontinental'. What do you make of them?"

✳ Solution on page 232 ✳

The Abbot

"I HAVE A HISTORICAL CURIOSITY FOR

you here Watson," Holmes told me one morning. "A little mental trial handed down through history from the 8th Century. The Abbot in question, one Alcuin by name, is famed amongst devotees of recreational mental exercise."

"An impressive feat."

"Very much. In this question, he suggests that 100 modia of corn are to be divided between 100 people, but rather than divide the corn equally, he mandates that each man should receive a triple share, each woman a double share, and each child a half-share. If you assume for the sake of argument that there are five times as many men as women, then you can tell me, undoubtedly, how many men, women and children there are in the group."

✱ Solution on page 233 ✱

PART THREE

CUNNING

✳ ✳ ✳

The Statuette

HOLMES SET ASIDE HIS NEWSPAPER

and looked up at me over breakfast one morning. "Do you suppose you have a head for business, Watson?"

"I dare say I'd be able to pick it up," I replied.

Holmes tapped the paper thoughtfully. "Let us suppose that you are a seller of antiquities. You have in your possession a rather pleasant statuette. A distinguished elderly gentleman comes in to your premises, and declares that the piece is familiar to him. He purchases it enthusiastically, not even blinking at your £100 price tag.

"Once the transaction is complete, the gentleman informs you that the piece is one of a pair; fairly valued by yourself as a singleton, but worth many times that amount if coupled with its mate. He offers to pay you a massive £1000 if you can obtain the other, and tells you his hotel. He leaves, and naturally you begin making enquiries about the statuette.

"Some days later, a fellow comes by with an identical companion to the statuette you sold. He says that he's heard you're looking for his piece, and is willing to part with it for £300. What say you? Does that sound like a good deal?"

What say you indeed?

❊ Solution on page 235 ❊

Cold Hands

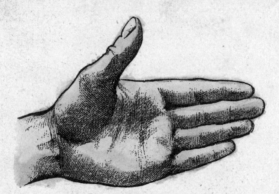

"I HAVE ANOTHER LITTLE THERMAL

question for you,"Holmes said to me.

"As you wish," I replied.

"Breathe slowly onto the palm of your hand. Yes, like so. How does it feel?"

"Well," said I, "warm and damp."

"Quite. Now repeat the process, but this time purse your lips and blow vigorously."

"The effect is considerably cooler," I said.

"But your breath – and your hand – are the same temperature on both occasions. So why the difference?"

❋ Solution on page 236 ❋

Dedication

I TOOK THE OPPORTUNITY, OVER A

luncheon of Mrs. Hudson's fine ham and sliced tomatoes, to take my turn in throwing a little unexpected riddle at Holmes. He was amused, if hardly baffled, so I feel it may be of some entertainment to you.

There is a shop which is devoted to the sale of one particular staple of daily life. It sells many varieties of this particular device, all of which serve exactly the same broad purpose. Some of these varieties are made up of tens of thousands of individual, moving pieces, whilst others consist of less than twenty such parts. A few are completely solid, immobile throughout, and yet still function as well as the most complex. They may likewise range in size from taller and heavier than a man down to being less than the size of a fingernail, but the very tiniest can still have more separate moving parts than the largest.

Can you guess the identity of this device?

❋ Solution on page 237 ❋

Grains of Sand

HOLMES, ONE MORNING, SOMEWHAT

startled me by producing an hourglass and waving it under my nose.

"Let's put your deductive mind to work, Watson. This hourglass has run its course. If I turn it over, so that the sand within it is flowing downwards, will it be minutely lighter on account of having some of its constituent parts in weightless free fall?"

I had to think about that for a moment.

❋ Solution on page 238 ❋

The Green Stone

HOLMES AND I WERE PURSUING

an unfortunate incident connected to the theft of the Green Stone of Harvington. The owners, Rupert and Rebecca Coynes, had come into its possession some years before. On the evening of the theft, the couple had met for refreshments at a London hotel when Rupert had a seizure and collapsed dead. It was later found that he had been poisoned, and mere blind luck had helped Rebecca avoid the same fate.

After the Stone's return, Rebecca had difficulty understanding why she had lived whilst her husband had died. They had both been perfectly healthy and followed a very similar diet. Both their drinks had been laced with identical amounts of toxin, and Rebecca's resilience and constitution was no different to her husband's. To her credit, she refused to believe that it was some divine providence that spared her, but understandably, the matter plagued her with considerable guilt.

Sherlock Holmes bore Rebecca's anguished confusion placidly, and when her tears had subsided, said "Tell me, were you thirsty that evening?" Rebecca nodded, obviously perplexed. Holmes smiled, and said nothing, and it was left to me to explain.

❊ Solution on page 239 ❊

The Sixth Curiosity

"MRS HUDSON INFORMS ME THAT

her greengrocer was unable to provide her with her usual 12" bundle of leeks at the market today, and instead gave her two 6" bundles."

———— ◆ ————

"Ah well," I said, my mind not on leeks.

"He had her pay a little extra as well, for the effort involved in making the two bundles."

"Seems reasonable enough," I said. But was it?

❋ Solution on page 238 ❋

The Cult of the Red Star

HOLMES WAS READING ONE OF HIS

penny dreadfuls. After a short time, be put the pamphlet down and sighed. "It is obvious," said he, "that the murder was committed by the victim's father's brother-in-law. Or the victim's brother's father-in-law. Or, I suppose, the victim's father-in-law's brother. I hate it when the case is so transparent."

It didn't sound in the least bit transparent to me, and I said so. "You yourself cannot even decide between three possible murderers."

"Nonsense," Holmes said crisply. "There is only one possible candidate, and I have identified him precisely."

What did he mean?

✷ Solution on page 240 ✷

Afternoon

"LET'S KEEP YOUR MIND ON ITS TOES,"

Holmes said to me as I was looking out of the window one afternoon.

───────◆───────

I made no protest, so he continued.

"How many minutes are we now before 6pm,
if fifty minutes ago it was four times as many minutes past 3pm?"

✳ Solution on page 240 ✳

Dimples

WE WERE WALKING IN HYDE PARK

one summery afternoon when I spotted a golf ball under the edge of a bush. I fished it out and had a glance at it.

"Look, Holmes, a guttie. One hardly sees a featherie any more, but they were all the thing in my father's day."

"Someone has been practising his putting," Holmes replied. "A short man, I'd say. But yes, the new balls totally outclass the old. It's not just the rubbery gutta-percha on the inside, however."

"Is it not?"

"You're not a golfing man. The dimples make the ball travel up to four times as far as an identical but undimpled specimen would."

"I've thought of taking it up," I said. "It may help me improve my physical condition. But why would dimples make such a dramatic difference?"

❋ Solution on page 240 ❋

Suffocation

LADY CASTERTON WAS FOUND SUFFOCATED

to death in her bedroom shortly after 7pm, when the maid went to discover why her employer had not appeared for dinner. From an examination of the body, it was clear that she had been killed a little after six at the very earliest. Suspicion naturally fell onto her nephew, her inheritor, with whom relations had been strained in recent weeks. He would have looked like a prime suspect, were it not for the testimony of the maid.

———— ◆ ————

"He left the house at 11 minutes to 6. I'm certain of it. I was in the drawing room, tidying. I heard him leave, clear as anything, and looked up to check the time. He doesn't usually depart before dinner, see? So I looked up at the clock, and thought to myself, 'Why, it's not even 10 to, yet.' So it can't be him. I won't see an innocent man swing."

With no other suspects or evidence of intruders, and the maid's physical weakness ruling her out, the police eventually turned to Baker Street for assistance. Holmes seemed interested briefly, but took a quick look inside the door, then called the maid over and asked her a single question.

Do you understand the situation?

❋ Solution on page 242 ❋

The Sixth Literal Oddity

ONE AFTERNOON, HOLMES HANDED ME

a scrap of notepaper. It bore a short list of words, like so:

uncopyrightable
dermatoglyphics
misconjugatedly
hydropneumatics

"One of your word puzzles," I surmised.

"Indeed," said Holmes. "Taken together, these words are the longest English examples of what, exactly?"

✻ Solution on page 243 ✻

The Sixth Mental Trial

WE WERE SITTING AT BREAKFAST

when Holmes said to me, "Let us return to my hypothetical friend for a moment, my dear Watson."

———◆———

"The wily Alfie."

"Just so. Today, he is joined by several members of his family – Fred, George and Harry. The four were sitting down to tea together, when Alfie noted that George had the same familial relationship to Fred as he himself did to Harry. Furthermore, Alfie himself had the same familial relationship to Fred as George did to him."

"A knotty matter."

"Can you untangle it?"

✳ Solution on page 243 ✳

Watch Out

"YOU KNOW THAT I HAVE NO GREAT

love of the Alps," Holmes said. We had been talking idly about skiers. "One of the lesser known perils is that it can be difficult to keep the precise time."

"You mean you get distracted?"

"Not a bit of it," Holmes replied. "Both our pocket watches are scrupulously accurate. If I were to go and spend a period of time up in the Alps, making sure to keep my pocket watch at a healthy room temperature at all times, when I returned here our watches would show a noticeable difference. Despite the fact that the accuracy of my watch should not have suffered one iota from the experience. Can you account for it?"

✳ Solution on page 244 ✳

Afghan Shot

I REMEMBER A PUZZLING PROBLEM

that I encountered courtesy of a fellow soldier in Afghanistan. He was the quartermaster, and was trying to take consignment of a box of small cannon shot, iron balls precisely two inches across. The crate that he had received was 14" in depth, 24⁹⁄₁₀" in length, and 22⅖" wide, and it was packed to the brim. Sadly, it neglected to list the number of balls it contained.

Can you deduce how many shot balls were in the crate?

✳ Solution on page 244 ✳

The Dinner Table

"MY HYPOTHETICAL FRIEND ALFIE IS
having a dinner party," Holmes informed me.

I prepared my brain as best I could for one of his typically baffling onslaughts.

"In addition to Bill and Charlie, he is also expecting Don, Eric, Fred and George."

"Quite a turn-out," I said.

"Alfie is setting places around a circular table, and wants to ensure everyone gets to sit next to everyone else, so he is having them change places between each of the three courses. He is however a little tired of George, and always fond of Bill. His intention is to arrange everyone around the table in alphabetical order for the starter. How should he arrange the men for the other two courses to ensure everyone sits beside everyone else, yet still keep Bill as close as that will allow, and George as distant?"

※ Solution on page 245 ※

The Bicycle

ONE AFTERNOON, AT MY MEDICAL PRACTICE,

I overheard a young patient attempting to extort a gift of a bicycle from her mother as a reward for the girl's good behaviour in complying with my ministrations. The mother was amused, as was I, but remained resolute.

"You can have a bicycle when you are exactly one third of my age, and not before. You are still too young, and I don't want you haring around on one of those things."

The little girl clearly deemed this acceptable, for she was perfectly sweet throughout her examination. I knew from my notes that she was 13, and her mother was 46. When I put the situation to Holmes, he was able to work out how long it would be before the girl got her bike in a flash.

Can you do so?

✴ Solution on page 246 ✴

Highland Fling

"SUPERSTITIOUS NONSENSE!"

Sherlock Holmes slammed his newspaper down on the desk in irritation.

I enquired mildly regarding the nature of the story that had aroused my friend's ire.

"It is in the nature of the weak mind to ever seek supernatural intervention in even the simplest of matters," he replied, more calmly. "This article spins a tale of a supposedly Highland marriage, and the supposed curse that has been inflicted upon it. All utter nonsense."

"Of course," said I.

"A young couple chose this Candlemas just past for their nuptials. As the ceremony was progressing, a local girl burst in to the church and declared that as she had been passed over by the groom, she had ensured that the marriage would be a doomed one. As a sign, the church bell would not ring to celebrate their union. She then consumed some poisonous concoction, and staggered back out in a suitably theatrical manner. She was later found dead."

"I say!"

"The ceremony resumed, but the entire wedding party was afflicted with horror when, at the climax, the Church bell did indeed fail to sound. The bride fainted dead away, and several other ladies had to be attended to. When the groom and his man went with the vicar to investigate, they could find no sign of tampering, and indeed the bell worked again thereafter. So, being feeble-witted, they all declared it had to be the work of the devil in league with the spurned witch girl, and the bride has barely eaten nor slept since."

It was clear Holmes had a different explanation in mind. Can you imagine what?

❋ Solution on page 247 ❋

Big Squares

HOLMES CORNERED ME NEAR THE WINDOW,

and expressed concern that his previous challenge to me involving the arrangement of each of the nine digits from 1 to 9 into a series of square numbers had not been stern enough.

———◆———

I tried to persuade him that I felt most mathematically enlightened,
but he was most insistent that I try again, this time to combine all of the digits into one single, massive square number. As if such a request were not enough, he casually added that it had to be the smallest possible such square.

I agreed as graciously as possible, and retired to my notepaper.

Can you find the answer?

※ Solution on page 247 ※

The Seventh Literal Oddity

"TELL ME, WATSON," HOLMES SAID.

"How many words in English use do you think there are that end with the letters -bt?"

"Well," I began, "there must be..."

"Careful man, give it a little thought."

I took his advice, and I'd suggest you do the same.

✳ Solution on page 248 ✳

The Switch

"OBSERVE THE TIME WOULD YOU,
Watson old chap?"

I did as instructed. "Just a little after 4.42, Holmes."

He nodded. "So when the positions of the hands are exactly reversed, it will be a bit after 8.23."

"Just so," I agreed.

"Given that the position of the hour hand is fixed precisely, moment by moment, by the exact movement of the minute hand, there are only a limited number of times in any given period when the positions of the hands will exactly swap locations. If it was 4.45, there would be no reverse alignment."

"I can see that," I said.

"So how many times do you think the hands of a clock will exactly reverse themselves between 3pm and midnight?"

✹ Solution on page 249 ✹

The Circus

IT WAS A CHILLY NOVEMBER EVENING WHEN

Holmes informed me that he had obtained tickets to attend a circus on Clapham Common that very night. I expressed a certain amount of surprise, given that he had never shown enthusiasm for such diversions.

———◆———

"Ah," said he. "I have had word that there may be some foul play afoot."

When we got there, we discovered a somewhat down-at-heel troupe, but none the less enthusiastic and committed for that. The performers included a small team of musicians and their conductor, a handful of clowns of various degrees of grotesqueness, a pair of aerial performers, a stage magician with assistant, two animal handlers, and the obligatory grandiose Ringmaster.

The performance was well-attended, and the audience seemed pleased enough as it unfolded along its predictable lines. During the trapeze act, something seemed to startle Holmes, and he snapped out of his inattentive reverie, leaning forward suddenly. Less than a minute later, tragedy struck. One of the trapeze artists mistimed his leap, and plummeted to the floor. The audience dissolved into a shrieking mass as the Beethoven screeched to a halt, and loud wails of anguish burst from the magician's assistant. I pushed my way into the ring, but it was hopeless.

"I'm afraid he's dead," I said to the horrified Ringmaster.

"Murdered," added Holmes, just behind me.

The Ringmaster and I spun round to look at him.

"Yes, murdered," Holmes said. "And we all watched the villain kill him, and did nothing."

What did he mean?

✳ Solution on page 250 ✳

The Third Portmanteau

I WAS TAKING MY EASE ONE EVENING

in Baker Street, following a rather delightful dinner of stuffed quail that Mrs. Hudson had prepared for Sherlock Holmes and myself. I had thought that Holmes was conducting some abstruse chemical experiment or other, but was disabused of that notion when he appeared beside me and wordlessly handed me a rather eccentric illustration, which I have diligently copied below.

I recognised it for what it was, of course. "This is one of your devilish picture puzzles," said I.

"I see nothing escapes you," Holmes replied with a twinkle.

"So I am to consider each separate element of the image as a clue, and deduce the only possible location that fits all the evidence."

"You are," Holmes agreed. "If you are so able. Restrict your considerations to London however, Watson."

I gave it some thought, and was finally able to pronounce a solution which Holmes would accept. Where does the picture refer to?

✳ Solution on page 251 ✳

Urchins

WIGGINS WAS WITH US, RECEIVING A

briefing for a sensitive mission of observation. Holmes was most insistent that he go to extraordinary steps to avoid detection.

"I want you to use nine lads, Wiggins. Send them out in groups of three. You'll need to have them venture forth for six days. To help avoid detection though, I do not want any two boys next to each other twice. You may place them in the same group a second time, so long as they are not adjacent to someone they have been adjacent to before."

"No problem, Mr. Holmes," said the urchin, "just as you like." He sounded confident.

Could you have matched Holmes' instructions?

❋ Solution on page 252 ❋

The Meadow of Death

"A COUPLE WERE FOUND DEAD IN A QUIET

valley in the Highlands," Holmes said to me one morning, apropos of nothing.

"They were murdered, I assume?" It was rather rare for Holmes to take interest in cases where foul play was not involved.

"It seems not," was his surprising reply. "They were found lying next to each other, hand in hand, in a pleasant field carpeted with new spring flowers. There was no sign of whatever it was that killed them. They were less than a mile to the nearest village. There was no evidence of any sort of murderous assault, no broken limbs, nor any of the tell-tale signs that suicide might have left. Lightning would have left char marks, rocks would have caused clearly visible wounds, and the physicians found no evidence of poisons or disease. They did not appear to have been robbed, either. I have an idea, of course. But what do you make of it?"

The Egg

"HAVE YOU THOUGHT MUCH ABOUT

eggs, Watson?" Holmes asked me during breakfast.

"I prefer them poached, given a choice."

"I really referred to the shape of the shell."

I mused on that for a moment. "Not especially," I admitted.

"Are you not curious as to why they are that particular drop-like shape, rather than being spherical, which would make them stronger?"

"I suppose it is an interesting question, yes."

"And what answer would you come up with?"

✻ Solutions on pages 252 & 253 ✻

The Eighth Literal Oddity

FINDING MYSELF AT AN IDLE MOMENT

on a quiet September afternoon, I asked Holmes if he happened to have any little word trial prepared which he had been saving up to vex me with. That may strike you as a little masochistic, but I was looking for a diversion.

He searched his memory for a moment, and nodded. "I'll offer you 'regimentations' and the mineral 'nitromagnesite'. What distinguishes them?"

✳ Solution on page 253 ✳

Gold

HOLMES AND I APPREHENDED A VICIOUS

gold-smuggler in Epping one nasty September evening. He was a particularly unpleasant sort, and it was a genuine pleasure to hand him over to Scotland Yard.

He had been in the middle of preparing a consignment of gold slabs for shipment to France – 800 of them, each one 11" wide, 12½" long, and 1" deep. A king's ransom indeed.

Holmes pointed out to my attention that the box he had packed them in was square, and sufficiently high that it exactly contained all of the slabs with no wasted space left over. Further more, less than a dozen of the slabs had been stood on an edge.

Can you discern the dimensions of the box?

✻ Solution on page 254 ✻

Stones

ONE PLEASANT SUNDAY AFTERNOON,

Holmes had the Irregulars gather him up a basket of precisely fifty stones. Then starting from the step of 221b Baker Street, towards St. John's Wood, Holmes started laying the stones out with an ever increasing gap between them. He placed the second stone one yard from the first, the third three yards from the second, the fourth five yards from the third, and the fifth seven yards from the fourth.

At this point, he returned to where the rest of us were standing, watching him curiously.

"Young Wiggins, what would you say if I told you that I would place all fifty stones according to this pattern, and then pay you a farthing to pick them back up – but strictly one at a time, bringing each back to the basket here at the start before going to fetch the next?"

"I'd tell you to bugger off, Mr. Holmes, Sir."

Holmes laughed. "Quite right too."

But why?

❋ Solution on page 254 ❋

Hudsons Tangled

"I'VE MENTIONED MY NIECE KATIE

to you, I believe," said Mrs. Hudson to Sherlock Holmes one morning.

"Indeed," said Holmes. "She works for the family with the eccentric twins."

"That's her. She has a younger sister, Alison. Their ages can be a bit of a tangle."

"How so?" I asked.

Mrs. Hudson smiled, and took a deep breath. "Counted together, they are forty-four years of age. Katie is twice as old as Alison was when Katie was half as old as Alison will be when Alison is three times as old as Katie was when Katie was three times as old as Alison."

Can you tell how old Katie is?

✳ Solution on page 255 ✳

The Seventh Curiosity

SHORTLY AFTER CHRISTMAS ONE YEAR,

I was relaxing and enjoying the season when Holmes' thoughts turned to the tragic Massacre of the Innocents, King Herod's vile infanticide which we remember on December 28th.

———◆———

"It is said," Holmes mused, "that after the deed, a number of the unfortunate mites were buried in sand, with only their feet sticking up to indicate their presence. How do you imagine that they told the boys apart from the girls, on such scant evidence?"

❋ Solution on page 256 ❋

Fencing

"A GOOD DETECTIVE MUST BE A

man of science, Watson."

I of course agree with this sentiment, and said so. Among the many things that my time with Sherlock Holmes has taught me is the paramount importance of even the most seemingly irrelevant physical clue.

"What do you know of the science of acoustics?"

"As much as any common lay-man," I allowed. "I'm confident in saying that the old folk myth about a duck's quack having no echo is utter bunk, and physically impossible besides."

"Imagine you are putting up wooden fence posts in a large field, perhaps to prepare an enclosure for sheep."

"Very well." I duly complied, painting the scene with a little light drizzle, and a hilly backdrop.

"When you start, near a stone building, you can hear a clear echo coming back to you. Later, near the middle of the field, the hammering noise you make is dull and flat. But later still, in another part of the field, you can hear a clear ringing noise. Do you know what could cause such an effect?"

❋ Solution on page 256 ❋

The Soho Pit

WE WERE WALKING THROUGH THE SOHO AREA

of London one morning, in search of one of Holmes' less reputable contacts. As we strolled down Dean Street, we passed a workman engaged in digging a hole for some purpose or other.

———————

"You, sir, are five feet and ten inches in height," Holmes declared to him.

The man nodded. "And when I've gone twice as deep as I am now, then my head will be twice as far below the level of the pavement as it is above it this instant."

Holmes told the fellow how deep his hole was going to be, and got a respectful nod in return. Could you have done so?

✷ Solution on page 257 ✷

The Seventh Mental Trial

"I HAVE DECIDED THAT TODAY I KNOW TWO

hypothetical men, my dear Watson. Alfie and Bill."

"As you wish, Holmes," I said. "What do they look like?"

"Fishmongers," said he.

"So. Alright, I'm picturing a pair of hypothetical fish-mongers."

"It matters little, in truth. The case is that Alfie has twice as many sisters as he has brothers, whilst his sister Mary has the same number of sisters and brothers. Bill, by comparison, has three times as many sisters as brothers, but his sister Nancy has the same ratio of brothers to sisters as Mary does. Assuming both have just the bare amount of siblings required to fulfil their conditions, who has the more brothers, Alfie or Bill?"

❋ Solution on page 257 ❋

The Hanged Man

A RATHER PERPLEXING CRIME HAD

prompted Scotland Yard to summon Mr. Sherlock Holmes and myself to Draper Street. A temperamental young artist of some promise had been found hanged, and the police were at a loss to explain the murder.

His absence around town having been noted, the young man had been discovered in his rooms, behind doors so firmly locked and bolted that it took three stout constables to batter them open. The window was similarly secure, and anyway, it looked straight down onto the road some four stories below. The body itself was hanging by a short cord from a light fitting in the ceiling, nothing but air and dark carpet beneath its booted feet. In fact, there was no object whatsoever in evidence that the young man could possibly have stood upon with which to take his own life.
The room was perfectly tidy, and the maid assured us that everything looked to be in its usual order, with nothing missing, and no additions. The police were certain that the killer had tidied up after the murder, but didn't know how he had exited the room.

Sherlock Holmes walked through the door, glanced around once, and snorted in derision. He knelt by the corpse, touched the carpet, and then rose again. "Really, Lestrade," he said, drying his fingers on his handkerchief. "You've excelled yourself this time. The situation is perfectly clear."

Would you consider it so?

❋ Solution on page 258 ❋

Happy Family

A BRIEF VISIT FROM MRS. HUDSON,

with a nice pot of tea, prompted Sherlock Holmes to unleash an unusually fiendish little puzzle upon me.

"Our redoubtable Mrs. Hudson believes her family to be a complicated tangle, but honestly she could be much worse off."

"Oh, really?" I asked, innocently.

"Very much so," Holmes said. "Imagine a family friend being presented with the children of a house as follows. First a boy and a girl are brought in, let us call them Amelia and Barney. The friend is informed that Barney is twice Amelia's age. Then a second girl, Charlotte, arrives, and brings the total of the girls' ages to twice that of Barney's. After her comes another boy, Daniel, and his presence brings the combined ages of the boys to twice that of the girls. The final clincher is the arrival of the last child, Emily, on the occasion of her 21st birthday. Her presence swings the age total back, so that the combined ages of the girls is again twice that of the boys."

"It sounds a beastly business."

"Particularly, my dear Watson, when I ask you to tell me how old each of the children are."

❋ Solution on page 259 ❋

The Barn

NORFOLK WAS THE SETTING FOR THIS

particular problem. Inspector Lestrade brought word to Baker Street
one chilly February morning that a colleague of his up in King's Lynn was
having persistent trouble with a raider who specialised in robbing the
warehouses of the shipping companies out there. The investigation had
been proceeding well, until a sinister incident unnerved the superstitious
local constabulary enough that help had to be sought. Perhaps inevitably,
the problem found its way to Mr. Sherlock Holmes.

The villain had struck on a snowy Friday night, and made off unseen with a
substantial quantity of goods. Witness statements suggested the villain had
headed west out of the town, and once the storm had abated, and dawn had
broken, the police found a crisp, deep hoof-print trail clearly leading over
the fields. They followed the prints to a disused barn, steeled themselves,
and threw open the door, ready to apprehend the thief.

The barn, however, was empty, save for a few small discarded bits of farming
equipment. The snow was deep enough that even a sparrow's passing would
be clearly noted. There were no drag-marks where prints could have been
eliminated. There were no other ways out of the barn. The raider had
ridden into the barn and vanished into thin air, according to the disturbed
constables, "like the very Devil himself."

Holmes listened to Lestrade's tale, and just arched an eyebrow, clearly
amused. The inspector's wounded expression simply made Holmes's eyes
twinkle all the more. Can you explain?

❋ Solution on page 260 ❋

A Hearty Drop

"MY HYPOTHETICAL FRIEND ALFIE,"

Holmes said, "wishes to divide a keg of ale equitably between Bill, Charlie and himself."

"I dare say he does," I retorted. "That undoubtedly explains his hat problem."

Holmes was unruffled. "The keg contains a whole six quarts, but the men find themselves with just a 2½ quart pail and a three-pint pickling jar, fortunately both perfectly clean."

"Can you not imagine them a hypothetical pint glass?"

"I cannot," Holmes replied. "That being so, can you tell me how they might most efficiently divide and consume the ale so that each gets his four pints?"

❋ Solution on page 261 ❋

PART FOUR

FIENDISH

✳ ✳ ✳ ✳

The Eighth Mental Trial

"MY HYPOTHETICAL FRIENDS, ALFIE AND BILL,

have an acquaintance," Holmes said to me one afternoon. I understood this to mean that he had another mental challenge for me.

––––◆◆◆––––

"Soon you will have an entirely hypothetical village," I said.

"That may happen, my dear Watson. But today, we are concerned just with the addition of Charlie. Poor Charlie has run out of lamp oil at an inopportune moment. Alfie and Bill both have reasonable stocks – Alfie has eight pints, and Bill has five. The two decide that the comradely thing to do would be to pool their oil, and divide it up into thirds. This they do, and to repay their kindness, Charlie hands over thirteen farthings."

"Who will be their next friend?" I asked. "David?"

"Unlikely," said Holmes. "But for now, in the interests of equity, tell me, how should the money be divided?

※ Solution on page 263 ※

In Paris

"YOU MAY RECALL THAT THE WORLD'S FAIR

was held in Paris a few years back," Holmes said.

---◆◇◆---

I nodded. "Quite the show."

"Quite. Did you hear about the missing brother?"

"No?" I leaned forward, curiosity engaged.

"A funny business. An American lady and her brother arrived at the Ritz the afternoon before the fair, and checked in to their rooms. They had dinner together, but the lady was tired, and her brother flat-out exhausted, so they called it an early night.

"The next morning, the lady was surprised that her brother did not appear at their agreed-upon time for breakfast. She asked the waiter if he had already eaten, and received just a puzzled stare. When she went looking for his room, number 13, she was unable to find it, and had to seek help from the staff. The concierge superciliously informed her that there was no Room 13. The manager, when he appeared, said the same. All the staff insisted she had arrived alone and eaten alone the night before. The registry book showed just her name. The rooms on the first floor went straight from 12 to 14. Despite her very great distress, she could find no evidence her brother had ever existed."

"My word," I said, perplexed.

"What do you suppose was going on?"

❊ Solution on page 264 ❊

Pop Pop

"HAVE YOU SEEN ONE OF THESE
before, Watson?"

Holmes handed me a small tin boat. It looked unremarkable at first glance, but on closer inspection, I discovered what appeared to be a small boiler set-up in the wheelhouse, and a pipe protruding out of the back. I admitted that the thing was unfamiliar.

"A clever Frenchman has designed it," Holmes said. "A child's toy. You prime the mechanism with a little water, light the small spirit burner, and then place it in a bathtub or paddling pool or what have you. Once the boiler has warmed up, the toy will propel itself across the surface. It accelerates in little fits and starts, emitting a popping noise as it does so."

"Ingenious," I said.

"Yes, quite. How do you imagine that it works? That pipe is the sole egress from the boiler."

✷ Solution on page 265 ✷

Evasion

"SEE IF YOU CAN DO SOMETHING WITH THIS

little bit of chronological evasion," Holmes said to me one afternoon.

"I'll try," I promised.

"A man and a woman are discussing their respective ages. Their combined age is 49, and they come to the conclusion that when the man was the age that the woman is now, he was at that time twice as old as she was."

"I see."

"Do you? How old are the pair now?"

❋ Solution on page 266 ❋

Six-Sided Dice

"A SIMPLE LITTLE QUESTION
for you, Watson."

Holmes tossed me a standard die, which I caught.

"The humble die conceals many mysteries and is at the heart of many adventures. Given that each pair of opposite faces on the die must always add up to seven, how many different ways are there to set out the numbers on three separate dice?

✳ Solution on page 266 ✳

The Ninth Literal Oddity

"ARE YOU READY TO GIVE YOUR MIND
a stern lexical test, Watson?"

I confessed that 'stern' sounded a little daunting, but so long as there was no dire penalty for failure, I was prepared to do my best.

"That's the spirit, old chap. The nine-letter word 'checkbook', an American coinage from our own 'chequebook', possesses an unusual quality. This is shared with a small number of other words, all shorter, including our very own 'exceeded'. What do you imagine that it is?"

✳ Solution on page 267 ✳

The Dictionary

I WATCHED CURIOUSLY AS HOLMES

fished a number of books out from the shelves in his study. The books were of a size, which I quickly determined had been the primary motivation for their selection. Holmes brought them over, and popped them down on the table at my elbow.

"You have here a stack of books, numbering half a dozen in total," he declared.

"Indeed so," said I.

"It is of course possible to edge the stack out slightly, so that the second book protrudes a little further than the first. I've placed the books up against the very edge of the table. Do you imagine that it is possible to arrange the stack I have provided you with in such a way that one – or more – of the books is hanging completely over the table?"

✳ Solution on page 268 ✳

The Eighth Curiosity

"GIRDLE THE EARTH!"

"What?" I snapped to attention, reasonably startled.

"In your mind, man. Girdle the Earth. With steel, I dare say, for structure. Now assuming – fallaciously, of course – that the Earth were perfectly flat and round around the equator so such a girdle could be circular, place it so that it is exactly flush with the Earth."

I complied.

"Now, if you added six yards to the length of that girdle, how far do you suppose that would raise it off the surface?"

✳ Solution on page 269 ✳

The Fish Murder

A REGULAR POLICE PATROL FOUND

Mister Frank Hale gasping his very last breath in the streets surrounding Billingsgate Fish Market in the early hours. He had been stabbed through the neck, and clearly it had happened very recently. On the basis that his killer had to still be nearby, the constables chased down and apprehended the only other fellow on the street.

———◆———

Like Hale, Rick Weir was a fish merchant, and the police were able to show that the pair were at least rivals professionally. Under questioning, Weir maintained total ignorance of the event, and claimed that he had fled the police simply out of an instinct born from confusion. As evidence of his innocence, he pointed out that he had nothing on his person that could remotely be used as a murder weapon, nor had he discarded any such item. The police searched the area thoroughly, but could find nothing that might have plausibly caused Hale's rather irregularly-shaped wound.

With nothing more to go on than the victim's damp shirt collar and ragged stab-wound, Scotland Yard was on the verge of allowing Weir his freedom. It was at that point that Holmes heard of the case, and scribbled a quick note to Inspector Lestrade. Weir was formally charged with the murder in less than an hour.

Can you imagine what thought had occurred to my companion?

❋ Solution on page 269 ❋

The Box

HOLMES TOOK DELIVERY OF A JAR

of chemicals, and once he had it stowed away safely, tossed the box to me.

I caught it automatically. It seemed a rather plain affair.

"That box has a top that is 120 inches square. The side is 96 inches square, and the end is 80 inches square. What are its dimensions?"

✳ Solution on page 270 ✳

Sheep

"SOMETIMES, MY DEAR WATSON,
you have to think outside the boundaries of the sheep pen."

"A curious turn of phrase, old friend."

"But deliberate," Holmes said. "You have four sheep pens of equal size. How would you place fifteen sheep to ensure that each pen contained the same number of sheep?"

I thought about it for a little while. "It seems impossible, without butchering a sheep."

"Such exertions are unnecessary," said Holmes, "but do not forget my earlier admonition."

✳ Solution on page 270 ✳

The Fourth Portmanteau

"I HAVE ANOTHER PICTURE
for you to puzzle over, Watson."

Sherlock Holmes passed me the extraordinary illustration which I have reproduced here.

"It contains all the visual clues you could possibly require to positively identify one particular spot in London. When you can place the relevance of each element of the picture, you will be able to allow no possible doubt regarding the location to which it refers. Be stout; the solution is not quite as obvious as some of the other images I have passed you."

I turned my attention from my friend to the drawing he had given me. To where does it refer?

❋ Solution on page 271 ❋

Get a Hat

"MY HYPOTHETICAL FRIEND ALFIE'S

dinner party had six guests," Holmes said. "That meant that there were seven hats. By the time it came to depart, the men were too wearied by their exertions at the table to take notice of which hat they obtained."

"No doubt," I replied. "I suspect any normal man would be fatigued by an evening in your prodigious mind, my dear Holmes."

"Perhaps," he replied. "But either way, the truth is that after all had left, no man had the correct hat, not even Alfie. How many possible variations are there of this mishap?"

✷ Solution on page 272 ✷

Nephews

WE WERE IN THE AREA NEAR KING'S CROSS

railway station one morning, pursuing a matter involving a larcenous baker's nephew. I should make it clear that the larceny was on the baker's part; the nephew was quite innocent. As that may be, I was deep in thought when Holmes said to me, "Watson old chap, do you know that it is possible to be both the nephew and uncle of a fellow at the same time?"

That brought me up short. "Surely not," I protested.

"Oh yes," Holmes said. "All perfectly within the law, too."

"How can that be?"

"Why don't you tell me," he replied.

✷ Solution on page 273 ✷

The Ninth Mental Trial

"I HAVE ANOTHER MENTAL EXERCISE

for you, my friend."

I looked up from my book. "Very well, my dear Holmes. I'm sure it is to my benefit."

"Immeasurably," came the reply. "Consider for a moment that you have been given a counterfeit shilling in amongst your money. It is ever so slightly lighter than it ought to be, but it is otherwise indistinguishable from the real thing. You cannot tell by hand, but you have a balance scale. What is the least number of weighings that you can perform upon the scale to discover the precise identity of the counterfeit?"

✳ Solution on page 273 ✳

Equity

"I HAVE AN AMUSING LITTLE TEST OF YOUR

mathematical faculties here, my dear Watson."

I suppressed a sigh, and girded my mental loins. "Indeed?"

"You may have noticed that the even digits, 2, 4, 6 and 8, add up to 20, whilst the odd digits, 1, 3, 5, 7 and 9, add up to 25. It's the unpaired 5 that makes the difference."

"I'm with you so far," I said.

"Excellent. Can you contrive a way to arrange these two sets of digits into additive sums which total an identical amount? You are allowed to use simple vulgar fractions if you wish, but nothing more complex than that, and the only mathematical operand available to you is addition."

"May I have some paper and a pencil?" I asked.

"Naturally," Holmes said.

What was the solution?

✳ Solution on page 274 ✳

Twenty Thousand Leagues

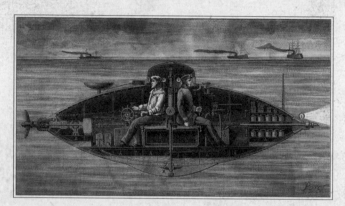

"AS I RECALL WATSON, YOU'VE READ

Mr. Verne's tale about Captain Nemo and his miraculous underwater submersible, the Nautilus."

I nodded. "I have. I enjoyed it, but I fear that it would offer you little. The villainies it contains have little mystery to them."

"So I gather," said Holmes. "Although I believe the French are currently testing a similar – if much less fanciful – device with a marked degree of success. I cannot help feeling that the captain of any such device would spend his entire time living in mortal terror of accidentally touching the bottom of the ocean."

"The risk of damage to the structure, you mean?"

"Well yes, there is that, but no, I was thinking of a danger that would apply to the mildest sandy bottom as much as to a jagged shelf. More so, even."

What did he mean?

✳ Solution on page 274 ✳

The Shoreditch Bank

SHERLOCK HOLMES AND MYSELF

encountered a cunning method of bank robbery in Shoreditch on one memorable occasion. The manager was diligent in his security arrangements. The bank's safe was a massive thing, complex enough that even a skilled thief would take an hour or more to get into it, and this with cutting tools that would leave very obvious scarring. This in turn was locked in the manager's office. The office door had a small viewing port set into in. The guards' rounds of the bank brought them past the manager's office every six minutes, and they always paused for a moment to peer through the port and inspect the safe.

Despite these precautions, when the cleaning lady went into the manager's office early on Monday morning, to start tidying up before the week began, she immediately realised that the bank had been burgled. The security men were utterly confounded, they and their colleagues having faithfully checked the safe every few minutes, all through the weekend. Given the length of time that it would have taken for the safe to be opened, and the regularity of the guards' observations, can you imagine how the criminals had found the time to get it open?

❋ Solution on page 275 ❋

Markham

"A VERY SIMPLE MATTER THIS ONE, WATSON."

Holmes indicated an illustration on his desk, which outlined the details from the scene of the recent Markham murder. "I feel confident that even you should be able to see through to the heart of the crime."

I reminded him that I was not familiar with the particulars of the case.

"Markham was in his study, working. His wife was in the drawing room, and has said that although her husband had been a little preoccupied recently, she had no idea that he was in danger. She realised that she could hear conversation through the wall: her husband sounding agitated, and a rougher man's voice which she could not clearly make out. Then there was a blood-curdling scream, a heavy thump, and silence. She rushed to the study door in a panic, but finding it locked on the inside, dashed out and around the side of the house to the study window. It too was locked tight, and the curtains drawn. Her statement is corroborated by the maid.

"Her cries for help brought the assistance of the police, who battered down the door and found the room as shown, and the window still firmly locked and barred from the inside. Markham was dead of course, with a hunting knife through his heart. Both the widow and the maid insist that no intruder could have escaped without their notice, and the police admit that they can find no signs of egress.

"So tell me. Who killed Markham?"

✳ Solution on page 276 ✳

Montenegro

HOLMES MADE THE ACQUAINTANCE

of a pair of charming rogues from Montenegro at one point, and, I gather, obtained all sorts of useful tid-bits from them. One of the items that he obtained was a curious little dice game.

The game is played with three regular six-sided dice. Each player selects two separate odd numbers that the three dice sum to. The four numbers must all be different, so in fairness, they take turns to select their numbers. They then throw the dice alternately; whoever throws one of their numbers first wins, although the opponent has one last chance to throw their own number and make for a draw.

The question is whether it is possible for the two players to have exactly identical odds of winning the game.

✳ Solution on page 277 ✳

Wordplay

"YOU MAY TAKE THE LETTERS FROM

A through to O," Holmes informed me suddenly.

"That's very kind of you," I replied. "But whatever do you mean?"

"I wish you to combine those letters into groups of three, so that no two letters ever share the same group twice. It is possible to form a clear 35 groups without any of them ever having a repeated letter pairing."

"Very well," I replied.

"That is not the challenge, however. The challenge is to form as many common 3-letter English words as possible within those 35 groups. Abbreviations and proper nouns are to be discounted, I'm afraid."

How well can you do?

✷ Solution on page 278 ✷

Wimbledon Common

HOLMES TURNED TO ME WITH A WRY SMILE

and tapped his Morning Post. "In here, Watson, we have the story of a cabbie who picked up a fare in Putney yesterday morning, took the fellow out into Wimbledon Common, and then bludgeoned him to death with a cudgel he kept under his seat. Why do you suppose he did so?"

"A vicious mugging?"

"Not so; the corpse was found with wallet and all effects."

"Some bad blood, then?"

"The two men had never even heard of each other before, let alone laid eyes on each other."

I thought for a moment. "Well, is the driver just demented?"

"Not a bit of it," said Holmes. "He is entirely rational, and has an explanation that he clearly feels justified his action. He will undoubtedly swing for it, although they might be more lenient if he were tried in Paris."

Can you guess what the reason was?

❋ Solution on page 279 ❋

The Tenth Mental Trial

"LET US RETURN ONE MORE TIME

to my hypothetical friends, Alfie and Bill. Imagine that you are with the pair of them in the office of a curious prison warder. Charlie's presence is not required."

"I am in prison with a pair of fishmongers," I noted.

"You are all innocent, of course," Holmes replied. "Sad victims of a miscarriage of justice, fear not."

"My mind is at ease."

"Capital. The warder shows you all five coloured signs, two black and three white. He then has you turn around in a line, and affixes a sign to the back of each of your prison uniforms. The warder informs you that the first man to correctly identify the colour of his sign will walk free; but identify wrongly, or collude, and your sentence will be extended. Then he allows you to turn around and inspect each other. You see that both Alfie and Bill are wearing white signs. The other two look at you, and at each other. What colour is your sign?"

※ Solution on page 279 ※

Most Irregular

IT WAS WIGGINS' PRECOCITY THAT FIRST

won him his exalted position at the head of the Baker Street Irregulars. When Holmes first encountered the urchin, he enquired as to the lad's age.

Rather than give a straight answer, the deviousness of Wiggins' reply earned Holmes' interest. "It's like this," he said. "The year I was born, David, the deacon now at Paddington Green, was just one quarter of the age of Father Anthony, and now he is a third of the age of Father Gary. I'm only a quarter as old as Father Anthony is now, but in four more years I'll be a quarter as old as Father Gary will be."

How old was Wiggins?

✻ Solution on page 280 ✻

Carl Black

"DID YOU SEE THE ITEM ABOUT THE DEATH
of Carl Black, Watson?"

"Who?"

"A former steel baron from New York. He was kidnapped last year by Serbian radicals during an exploratory business trip to the area, and ransomed for a very princely sum. He was lucky. Many such victims are never returned. Black resigned from the company immediately afterwards, although of course the firm's travel insurance covered the actual cost, and he moved to the south of France."

"Was he murdered?"

"No. Boating accident. A bit of foolishness, with serious consequences, but nothing in the least bit sinister about it."

"Oh," I said, increasingly mystified.

"Note that Black's former company was in good financial shape for the first time in five years, and that although relations were cordial, he had possessed no formal ties to them for almost twelve months. The interesting question then becomes, why was his former business partner caught trying to burn down Black's chateau three nights later?"

A good question.

❊ Solution on page 281 ❊

A Matter of Time

"COME, WATSON," SAID HOLMES TO ME

one afternoon. "Indulge me in a little matter of creative thought."

"Of course," I replied, with just a hint of trepidation.

"Suppose you need to exactly measure the passage of 45 minutes before making a timely entrance. You are required to wait in some dreary room, without a pocket-watch or convenient clock. You do, however, have two lengths of tallow-dipped stick, and a box of matches. The sticks are certain to burn for an hour precisely, but they will not do so at a constant rate.

"Variations in thickness and other defects of construction mean that after 30 minutes, just a small length of stick may be consumed, or alternately a great length. There is no guarantee that the pattern will be the same from one stick to the other. Yet these inadequate sticks are all you have at your disposal. How then would you use them to measure the time correctly?"

How indeed?

❋ Solution on page 282 ❋

The Faulty Watch

"LET US SUPPOSE YOUR WATCH IS FAULTY,
my dear Watson."

"You know very well that it is not," I replied.

"I do indeed, but for the sake of discussion, let us pretend that it is so."

"Very well."

"You have made some notes, and you are aware that the minute and hour hand on your watch meet precisely once every sixty-four minutes. Is your watch gaining time, or losing it?"

✳ Solution on page 282 ✳

The Final Portmanteau

"ANOTHER OF YOUR DAMNABLE

images, Holmes?" My eager expression removed any sting the words might have seemed to carry. The truth was, I rather enjoyed poring over the things.

———◆◆◆———

"Yes indeed, old friend. This one should provide you with a genuine challenge, too. Each aspect of the picture is a carefully-crafted clue. Taken together, all the clues point to just one place in London. This is the last of them for now, so I have naturally saved the best for the occasion."

He handed me the drawing, which I have replicated for you to examine. "Thank you, Holmes."

"You are of course welcome, but I'd not be too hasty. You may be cursing me before you solve this one."

It took a while, but I did indeed crack the mystery. Can you?

✳ Solution on page 283 ✳

The Ladies of Morden

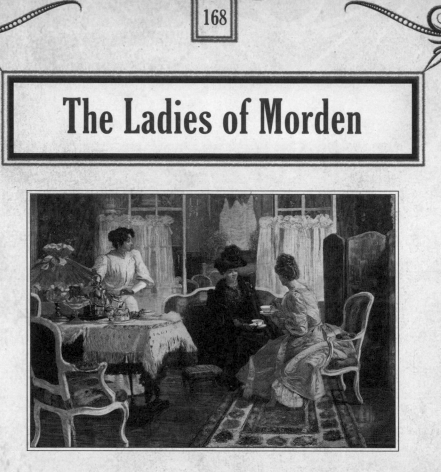

THE LADIES OF THE MORDEN WHIST CIRCLE

came to our attention in regard to a daring little robbery that had occurred in Balham. The case was solved easily, but Holmes was more interested in their playing regimen.

There were twelve ladies, and they so arranged themselves that over eleven evenings, each of them played no more than once with the same lady as a partner, nor more than twice with the same lady as an opponent. By this, they managed to ensure that every member played every other member in all possible quadrants.

Can you work out how such a thing might be achieved?

✳ Solution on page 284 ✳

The Final Curiosity

"TELL ME, WATSON. DO YOU IMAGINE
that a perfect billiard table is absolutely level?"

———◆———

"Of course," I replied.

"Oh? How curious. Would you like to guess why you are wrong?"

✳ Solution on page 285 ✳

Groups

ONE EVENING I FOUND MYSELF BETWEEN

relaxations, and Holmes seized the opportunity to spring a rather devilish little mathematical oddity upon me. All in the name of improving my mental acuity, you understand.

———— ◆ ————

"Take the nine digits," he instructed me. "Set them out once and once alone in three groups – a single digit, and two groups of four digits. Taking each group as a number, the groups must obey the stricture that the first group multiplied by the second group will equal the third group. Some methodical enquiry will be required."

Can you find the answer?

3 9 5
7 8 4
6 2
1

The Eggtimer's Companion

IN THE COURSE OF THE RATHER ODD AFFAIR

of the Eggtimer's Companion, Holmes and I came across a pair of feuding families in Highgate, the Adamses and the Southwells. Both families consisted of a mother, father and two children, and it was interesting to note that the sum totals of the ages of each family was 100 years.

The coincidence was increased by the fact that in both families, the daughter of the house was older than her brother, and if you added the squares of the ages of the mother, daughter and son together, you would get a total which exactly matched the square of the age of the father.

Miss Southwell was one year older than her brother however, whilst Miss Adams was two years older than hers. Armed with that knowledge, Holmes maintained, it was perfectly possible to discern the age of each of the eight individuals.

Can you deduce the ages?

❋ Solution on page 286 ❋

The Final Mental Trial

"I'D LIKE YOU TO CONSIDER THE FOLLOWING

sequence of numbers, Watson. They are: 2, 5, 8, 11, 16, 14. What number less than 20 is the next in the line? I assure you that you do not need any mathematical aptitude to arrive at the correct answer."

2, 5, 8, 11, 16, 14 ...

❋ Solution on page 286 ❋

Cones

HOLMES APPROACHED ME ONE LUNCHTIME

bearing a simple conical funnel and a determined expression. "I have a little trial for you, my dear Watson."

"By all means," I replied.

He passed me the cone. "If this funnel were a solid cone, it would be possible to whittle a straight cylinder out of it by removing the top, and then cutting straight down from the circular intersection."

"Very true," I observed.

"If I cut near the bottom, I would get a short, thick cylinder. If I cut near the top, it would be tall and thin."

"Yes, I can see that."

"So where would I cut to get the cylinder of the greatest volume?"

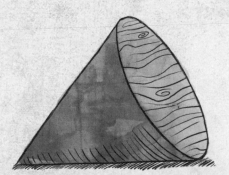

✳ Solution on page 286 ✳

Down on the Farm

I REMEMBER ONE PARTICULAR OCCASION

that pulled Holmes and myself out to an uninspiring pasture in West Sussex. A local farmer had noticed his sheep behaving oddly, and on investigation discovered a body in the middle of his field, in seemingly undisturbed grass. The body had been moved, but of course we had to slog out through the summer sun to examine the site. While we were looking around, Holmes discovered the top half of an unlit match, which he declared to have come from the corpse by dint of position and freshness.

A short while later, we got to examine the body itself, which had been moved to a more suitable location. He had been a middle-aged fellow, clearly of some means. Cause of death appeared to be general physical trauma, which included crushed ribs, smashed jaw and broken legs as well as the skull damage which had most probably finished him. He was dressed in soft shoes, stout woollen trousers and a sturdy leather jacket trimmed with fur. He had no personal possessions however, not even a watch.

Holmes took one look at his bootlaces and declared the man to be a Prussian, and then remarked that the style of his hair indicated he had been passing himself off as British, so he was probably a spy.

So declaring, he then asserted that the reason – and method – of his death were painfully obvious. Can you work out what he meant?

✳ Solution on page 287 ✳

Board

"I SAY, WATSON." I LOOKED UP

from my book. "Yes, Holmes?"

"I have a little challenge for you, simple in the telling, but less so in the execution. There are 64 squares on a chessboard, but how many different squares and rectangles can one or more of those squares be formed into?"

❋ Solution on page 287 ❋

The Night Watchman

WE WERE CALLED TO THE SCENE OF A

violent robbery down by the Thames, where a hapless night watchman had been murdered, and a consignment of shipped goods stolen. The poor watchman was dumped in the river after being killed, and the water immediately caused his pocket watch to stop working.

That would have given the time of the robbery, had one foolish policeman not tried to get the watch working again, and scrambled the time. Holmes was furious of course, but all the unfortunately constable could recall was that the second-hand had just passed 49, and that the hour and minute hand were perfectly aligned together.

Holmes recognized that the hands on the watch were of the constantly sweeping variety, rather than the type which clicks from division to division, and declared that this made the time of the robbery perfectly obvious.

What was the time on the watch when it stopped?

✳ Solution on page 288 ✳

The Final Literal Oddity

"I HAVE SAVED THE BEST FOR THE END,"

Holmes declared.

I felt my eyebrows raise. "What's that?"

"One final trial of your authorial muscle, Watson."

"Ah. If it is anything like the last..."

Holmes shook his head. "Not a bit of it. This one will genuinely tax your ingenuity."

"Very well," I replied, with a little trepidation.

"I want you to find me an English word which has each of its letters repeated exactly three times. I'll warn you now that I know of only one, and its etymology suggests an Italian derivation. I would discount any contrived word which was simply the same syllable repeated three times as being an unworthy answer."

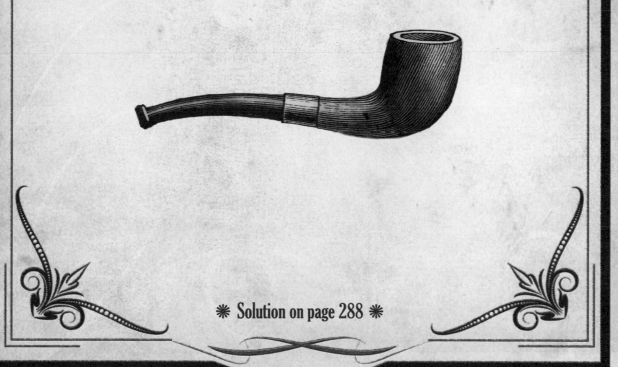

❋ Solution on page 288 ❋

Intersection

WALKING THROUGH CHARING CROSS,

Holmes drew my attention to a pair of wires. Each was fastened to the top of one pole, and ran straight down to the foot of the other.

***

"Those poles look to me to be five and seven feet high," Holmes declared.

"I dare say you're correct," I replied.

"Can you tell me how high off the ground the wires are when they intersect?"

"Possibly. How far apart do you think the poles are?"

"My dear Watson," Holmes said, "I assure you that is completely irrelevant."

What do you think the answer is?

❋ Solution on page 288 ❋

ANSWERS
AND SOLUTIONS

PART ONE

ELEMENTARY

✳

A MATTER OF IDENTITY

"It is vital to set aside your preconceptions if you are to think freely, Watson. It is the single most important step in accurate deduction. Make no assumptions that the evidence does not clearly support. Louise and Lisa have another sister, Lucy, likewise the product of the same pregnancy. They are not twins because they are in fact two out of three triplets."

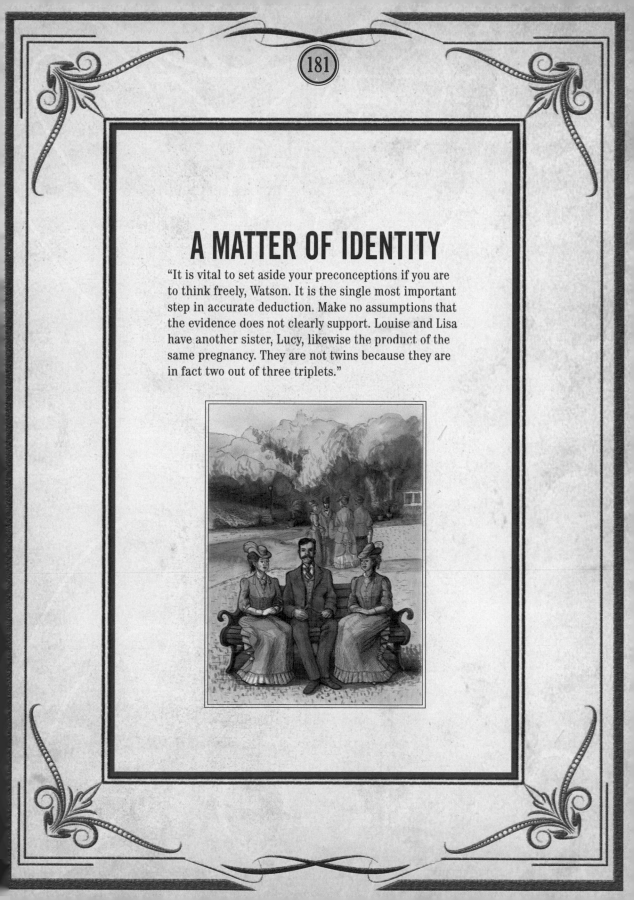

A DIFFICULT AGE

"Our chap's birthday is New Year's Eve, Watson, and our singular day is January 1st. Two days ago, on December 30th, he was 25. The next day, he attained 26. Today is the start of the new year, and at the end of this year he will become 27. At the end of the following year, therefore, he will be 28."

COLD FEET

Once I'd had a moment to actually consider the matter, the answer was obvious, given my medical experience. It is an issue of thermal conductivity. Ceramic tile, like metal, conducts heat very effectively; wool does so very poorly. So when you step on wool, the material is slow to leech the heat away from your foot. By comparison, when you step on tile, it draws the heat away quickly. So your feet stay warm on the carpet, and chill rapidly on ceramic, and you perceive the difference as the materials being different temperatures, even though they are not.

THE FIRST CURIOSITY

It is possible, but it would not be wise. The house would have to be located precisely upon the North Pole. Such a dwelling would be very cold indeed, and immensely inaccessible.

THE FOOL

Idiot or not, the villager clearly understood that the story of his poor decision-making was the source of a steady, if modest, income. By invariably taking the smaller coin, he ensured that his eccentric legend continued. If he were ever to take the larger coin, it would probably be the last one he claimed, so he continued to accept the smaller, knowing that over time he'd be far the better off for it.

RABBIT RACE

Given the consistency of the various times involved, the first three quarters of the race took exactly ¾ of the time — and the whole race took 9 minutes.

THE BARREL

"What you need to do is to tip it on its side just far enough that the water touches the lip of the barrel," Holmes told me. "Then look inside. If any of the bottom of the barrel is visible, then it is more than half empty. If any of the side wall is obscured, it is more than half full. If the water is exactly at the join, then it is in the precise half-way state."

"And would that be half-empty or half full?" I asked.

Holmes did not deign to reply.

———————————◆———————————

THE FIRST MENTAL TRIAL

Holmes was, of course, referring to my name.

WHISTLER

"Something to do with the temperature of the water, clearly," I said.

Holmes nodded. When I failed to continue immediately, he stepped in. "Liquids do not change to gas all at the same moment, nor does water heat evenly. As the water heats up, currents of heat encourage tiny bubbles of water vapour to form. These rise, being lighter than the water, and although some steam starts to issue, most of them encounter colder spots and collapse back into water. These little implosions, taken together, make the noise that you hear as the water heats. As it gets closer to boiling point, more and more of the tiny bubbles survive, and the number of implosions drastically decreases – so you get more steam and less sound. And then the water boils."

"Amazing," I said.

THE FIRST LITERAL ODDITY

As I'm sure you must have noticed, each word has the distinction of alternating consonant with vowel. I have since discovered that the terrible honorificabilitudinitatibus is the longest word in English to do so, with 27 letters to its count, although the others that Holmes mentioned are in joint seventh place at 15 letters in length.

ELEMENTARY GEOMETRY

You need to make the distance as effective as possible, and the means to do so is as follows.

First, plot the relative positions of the warehouse and the dock entrance, which are not in your power to alter, and then put in the river. Now, extend a line from the warehouse directly to the river, so that it hits it precisely on the perpendicular, make a note of that distance, and continue the line on past the river exactly the same distance again.

You may think of that as a reflection of the warehouse on the other side of the river.

From that point, extend a second line directly to the dock entrance. The place at which the second line crosses the river is the point that gives the shortest route from warehouse to river to entrance.

The solution works because obviously, any spot on the river is the same distance from the warehouse as it is from it's reflected spot on the other side. A straight line from the reflected point to the dock entrance is the shortest distance – and that marks the spot on the river bank that is the most efficient. What is the shortest distance from the reflected warehouse is also the shortest distance from the real one.

THE MEAL

For all his encyclopaedic knowledge, Holmes possessed some notable blind spots. When I first met him, he even went so far as to claim that he did not care whether the Earth revolved around the Sun or vice versa. Cosmology was always a weakness.

The woman was Eve, and the man Adam. He accepted the forbidden fruit from her, and in eating it, earned the divine judgement of mortality. If he had not eaten, he would have remained eternal. Holmes, naturally, was not in the least bit amused, but I must confess that I did derive some small measure of satisfaction from the incident.

EUREKA

The water level would fall, rather than rise or remain the same. Floating, the lump of steel displaces water equal to its weight; immersed, it displaces water equal only to its volume, and if it is heavy enough to sink, it is denser than water, and therefore its volume of water is less than its weight of water. It simply takes up less space, allowing the water level to sink.

REGENT STREET

The tardier man painted more lamp-posts, compensating for the earlier fellow's three by completing six. So the discrepancy is three – but this must be applied to each side. The tardy fellow did three extra; the early one three too few. Therefore the tardy man painted six more posts.

RIDER

The answer is not 10mph, although it is tempting to think it should be.

Let us say the journey is 24 miles. The outward journey, then, is 2 hours, and the return is three. The average speed then is found by adding 12+12+8+8+8, and dividing by 5, giving you a speed of nine and three fifths miles per hour.

Now consider a journey twice as long. Your average speed will be four hours at 12mph + six hours at 8mph, divided by the ten hours taken in total – or, again, nine and three fifths miles per hour.

So as you can see, the distance is irrespective. You take longer at the slower speed, and this skews the average below the more intuitive even division between the two.

THE SECOND MENTAL TRIAL

Holmes was right, it was fairly elementary.
The midpoint around the clock between 3am and 3pm
is 9am. Three hours after 9am is midday.

THE GANG

"I assume," Holmes said, "that you took no action
because no laws had been broken."

"Well..," began Lestrade.

"Tell me, were the firemen rescuing a pet or a child? I
suspect the latter, since they handed the unfortunate
to the wife."

Lestrade gave up. "An infant."

THE HAMPSTEAD TWINS

The children were born on a cruise liner heading from America to Japan. The elder was born shortly before hitting the International Date Line on March 1st; the younger was born a little after crossing it, when the date had gone back to February 28th.

Thus officially, the younger twin was born the day before her brother. During leap years, that gap stretches to two days.

THE FIRST PORTMANTEAU

The location in question is Her Majesty's Royal
Palace and Fortress, famed worldwide as the Tower of
London. The heart of the place is the White Tower, a
square moated keep, although the moat is now dry. The
Tower is guarded by Yeoman Warders, known popularly
as Beefeaters, and contains the Queen's Crown Jewels.
Ravens also guard the tower, and it is said, Heaven
help us, that if they ever fled, the British monarchy
would collapse.

THE THIRD MENTAL TRIAL

Alfie sat only in the second half of the journey. In that
section, he had to get up when he had half as far to go
as he had already travelled – or, in other words, he had
sat for two parts of that half of the journey, with one
remaining. So he was seated for 2/3 of the second half
of the journey – or 1/3 of the whole thing.

CATFORD

The teacher, who does not bow back, serves to
counterbalance the fact that each child is not required
to bow to his or herself. There are 900 bows, and
each child bows once for each other, so there are 30
children, as the square root of 900. As one third are
boys, then there are 10 boys, and 20 girls.

THE SECOND CURIOSITY

The obvious truth, of course, is that the distance between England and France varies quite wildly. Between Dover and Calais, it is just 21 miles, but the island of Guernsey, which is undeniably twixt the pair, is 26 miles from the English shore.

TRAINS

Despite what you may think, you do not need to know the duration of the journey in advance. For any given ratio of speeds, there is only one spot where the trains coincide, and this will fall in a different relative place. If the trains meet in the middle, they are going the same speed, and have the same time to destination. If one is going ten times as fast as the other, then when they meet, it will be impossible for the faster to have one hour to go and the slower to have just four hours left. In fact, as you can quickly verify for yourself, the one is running just twice the speed of the other, and they have been travelling for two hours already.

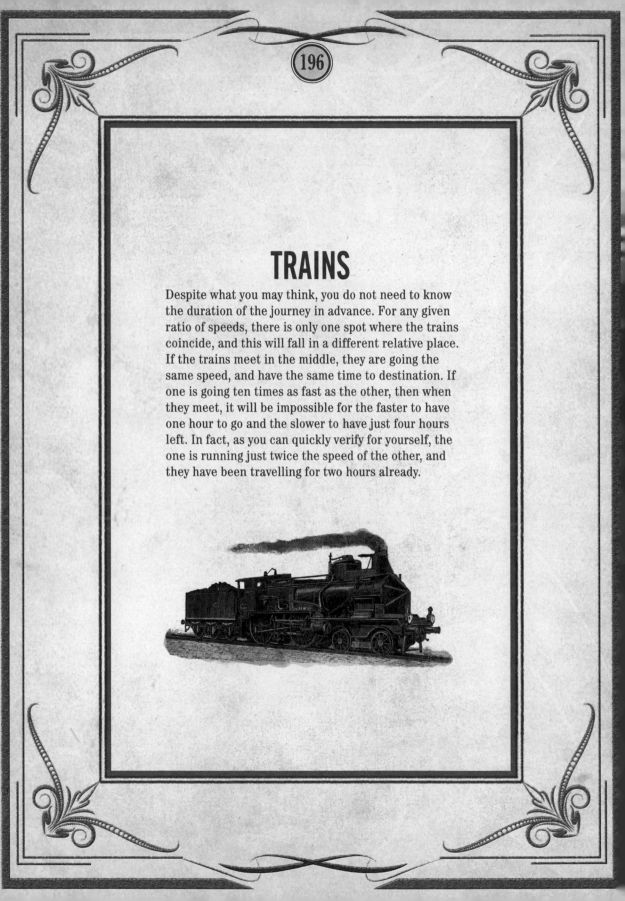

OVAL

Once Holmes showed me the trick, I realised that it was a matter of great simplicity. All you need to do is to place your paper upon a cylindrical surface. The difference in height will form the oval for you.

GLOUCESTER

Whatever the exact amounts of the liquids, provided that there is sufficient of each to complete all three steps, the answer will be the same. The fellow is halving the amount of milk in the first step, by doubling it with water, and then doubling the remaining water with the half-strength blend. The final step does not affect the contents of the larger barrel. The liquid is just one-quarter milk.

WIGGINS

After a suitable time, during which I did not honestly try to beat the lad out of his pittance, I flipped him his farthing, and informed him he had won.

"The letter 'U'!" he told me proudly.

"I didn't know you knew your letters," I said, somewhat surprised.

"Ah," said the lad. "You can thank Father Gary on Paddington Green for that."

I'm still not sure to this day if he meant for the riddle, or for literacy.

TO CATCH A THIEF

For every five strides of Holmes', the thief was taking eight, but those eight were equivalent to just three and a fifth of the taller man's. So Holmes was gaining one and four fifths of one of his strides for every five he took. The burglar's 27-stride lead is equivalent to ten and four fifths of Holmes' strides, and it will take exactly six gains of one and four fifths strides for Holmes to catch his quarry.

So Holmes has to take just 30 paces to catch the villain - who, in that time, will have run a total of 75 steps.

THE SECOND LITERAL ODDITY

Consisting solely as they do of the first seven letters of
the alphabet – they are in fact the joint longest words in
English to do so – both cabbaged and fabaceae are words
that can be played as a sequence of notes upon a musical
instrument.

CHEAPSIDE

There are two possible answers to the question. The fellow could have been either Holmes' uncle or his father.

THE THIRD CURIOSITY

The answer is, of course, £13,212.

WALKER

The trick to remaining upright on a high wire is
to keep your centre of gravity directly in line with
the rope as low down as possible. The long bar that
such performers use provides two handy functions.
It is long and heavy, so it possesses considerable
inertia. If a performer is wavering to one side, he can
push the bar in that direction, and get a stabilising
counter-push. More importantly however, the bar
has its weight concentrated towards the ends, which
dip down and serve to bring the performer's centre
of gravity down, ideally below the level of the rope
itself. With a centre of gravity below the rope, the
performer is far more stable, and much safer, than it
may otherwise appear to the untrained eye.

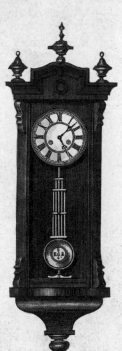

SWINGING PENDULUMS

"Nothing," Holmes said. "It wouldn't make the slightest bit of difference. The mass of the bob has no effect on the swing, as the whole thing is driven by gravity, which treats all objects as completely equal. Resistance from the air might play a part, if the experiment were not being conducted in a vacuum.

RICE

Holmes then informed me that rice is significantly more absorbent than salt, and droplets of moisture will naturally be drawn to it. As a result, the salt will remain dry. I confess that whilst I see his point, I'd rather not have to be picking bits of rice off the salt-spoon every time I use it.

THE BOARD

The meeting comprised of eighteen individuals. If three people mark the difference between half and two thirds, then the total is six times that number.

AN ISSUE OF AGE

To keep the difference in their ages down to as small a fraction as an eleventh of the total, the two digits of each age must be close together. Furthermore, the total age must be divisible by 11. As it transpires, the total has to be 99, and the couple's ages 54 and 45, the latter being the lady's age.

ALMONDS

With a little calculation, you can see that in each cycle, the youngest received nine almonds, the middle one got twelve, and the oldest had fourteen. The sum of these totals, 35, goes into 840 some 24 times. 28/35 is four-fifths, which means that the ages of each child are four fifths of the number of almonds each gets in a round. So the youngest is 7 and one fifth years old, the middle one is nine and three fifths years, and the eldest is 11 and a fifth years.

THE FONTAIGNES

Lord Fontaigne was three times his wife's age when they married. For him to now be twice her current age, he must have gone from three times her original age to four times, and she must have gone from her original age to twice that. In other words, her age in years is the same as the period of time it has taken for the ratio of their ages to go from 3:1 to 2:1. Lady Fontaigne was 19 when she married, and her husband 57; now she is 38, and her husband is 76.

PART TWO

STRAIGHTFORWARD

✳ ✳

THE SIGNPOST

"The matter is exceeding simple," Holmes said.
"You only have to pick the signpost up and point the
Mercaston sign in the direction which you have just
come from. Then all the other signs will of necessity
fall into their customary positions, and you can easily
discern the correct path to your destination."

WATER INTO WINE

Consider first the large glass. It contributes a third of its size of wine, and two thirds of water. The smaller glass is equal to a half of the large one, so it contributes an effective quarter-glass of wine, and a quarter-glass of water. Therefore we have a third plus a quarter of wine, and two thirds plus a quarter of water. Multiply these values out so that they are measured in equal twelfths. That is then 4 + 3 twelfths of wine, compared to 8+3 twelfths of water – or seven eighteenths of wine, to eleven eighteenths of water. We end up totally in eighteenths rather than the twelfths we converted to because there is a glass and a half of liquid.

ALBY

Holmes considered the matter carefully for a moment.
"It is clear that your cousin is an exemplary employee,
so obviously he is not at work during his daytime rest.
I assume therefore that he works the night-shift, and
lives in a converted cellar or some similar basement
abode that he has to walk down to get in to."

Mrs Hudson seemed genuinely delighted to have her
riddle seen through so swiftly.

THE THIRD LITERAL ODDITY

The words in question have all their letters arranged
in alphabetical order – or, in the case of spoonfeed,
reverse alphabetical order. As a point of interest,
Aegilops is the longest such English word in the usual
direction, and spoonfeed the longest going backwards.
If you prefer to exclude words with consecutive
repeated letters from the prize, then sponged and
wronged must unseat poor spoonfeed.

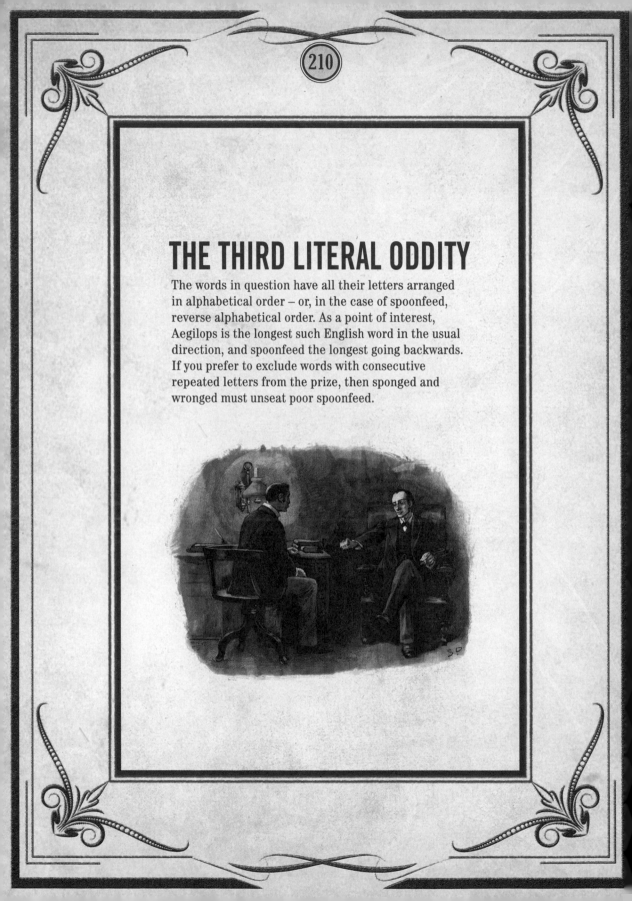

THE TIME

Regula Falsi, the technique of trying various solutions on a speculative basis, works nicely for this puzzle. Say it's 8pm. Then a quarter of the time from noon is 2hrs, and a half of the time to the following noon is 8hrs. The total is 2hrs too much. Try 9pm, giving you 2.25hrs before and 7.5hrs after. That's 9.75hrs, or 45 minutes too much. So an hour extra is worth 1.25hrs. You need to decrease the gap by .75 hrs. 0.75/1.25 is 0.6, or 36 minutes. The time is 9.36pm. A quarter of the time from noon is 2h 24m, and half the time to next noon is 7h 12m, or 9h 36m when added together.

THE FOURTH CURIOSITY

Of course, it does nothing of the sort. If you have three fourths, then a fourth is one third of that amount, not a quarter.

A VERY HUDSON CHRISTMAS

The smallest party that fits that description is just seven
people – a married couple, the father's parents, and the
couple's three children, two girls and a boy. Mrs. Hudson
needs to set eight places, including herself.

DRIFTS

The answer lay in the passage of the wind. A large, flat
surface such as the side of a house is going to divert
the wind quite considerably. It has to break quite some
distance before the house, in order to flow around it, and
this prevents a reasonable percentage of the snow from
being flung against it. This is not the case with something
as small – and rounded – as a telegraph pole, so the pole
gets proportionately more snow driven onto it.

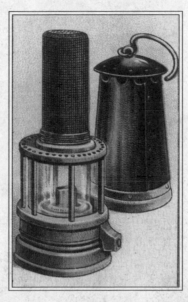

DAVY

"The fact of the matter is that the fine mesh disrupts the flames too much to permit them to escape its confines. The holes in the mesh are too narrow to allow it to propagate without losing all cohesion. It is vital to maintain the mesh in perfect working order however; even one broken link may be enough to spoil the effect."

THE FOURTH MENTAL TRIAL

Alfie is 40. His age plus six years is equal to five fourths of his age minus four years. This means that in terms of sheer values, four times his age plus 24 is equal to five times his age minus 16. Add 16 to each side, and four times his age plus 40 is the same as five times his age, or, simply, he is 40 years old.

SUFFOLK

By judicious use of Pythagoras's theorem, and the observation that the direct line from Gosbeck to the Crowfield-Hemingstone road cuts the route into a pair of right-angled triangles, the puzzle will quickly fall to our analysis. The direct line from Gosbeck to the road I should have taken is 12 miles, forming the longer line of the triangle with Crowfield, and the shorter line of the triangle with Hemingstone. The sum of the two hypotenuse values is 35, and from this, it is rapidly clear that the distance from Crowfield to Hemingstone is 25 miles.

THE FIRE

After I finally conceded that I would probably be burnt, Holmes pointed out that the correct course of action was to set another fire, a short way down from the unburnt end. Because the wind is blowing in a fixed direction, the new conflagration will be driven in the same direction as the current one. In its wake, the new fire will leave burnt ground. As it proceeds, I would be able to follow it onto the charred area, and when the larger flame front arrived, it would be unable to get purchase in this space. Thus I would create for myself an island of safety – from the flames, anyway.

THE WILL

To unravel the issue, Holmes looked at the apparent intent of the dead man. This was quite clearly that a son should get twice the sum of the widow, who in turn should get twice the inheritance of a daughter. The answer was to divide the estate by sevenths, and give one portion to the girl, two to the mother, and four to the son.

MODESTY

With 21 years between the eldest and youngest sibling, the girl must be 24, and her brother just 3.

THE HOUSE

As it transpired, the young woman had been hired chiefly for her similarity of appearance to her employer's daughter. The unfortunate girl had begun a romance with the small fellow, a sailor, and the father was violently opposed. Whilst his daughter remained unmarried, he had the use of her inheritance from her deceased mother – the lady of the house was therefore the girl's new stepmother.

The father decided to send the sailor a dismissive message, and then confine his daughter in a small room at the top of the house. Holmes' client was there to provide the false appearance of all being as usual. Apart from our client's original hair style, the two young women were of a type, and the activities the couple had her perform were such as to give the daughter's beau the impression that life without him went on pleasantly. He didn't believe a word of it, of course.

It all ended well enough, with the lovers free of interference and married, and our client gratifyingly unmolested.

THE BEACHCOMBER

Holmes explained that it was the sand of
the beach which caused the intense burnt hue. He
was of the opinion that sunlight reflected off the sand
far more effectively than off grass, stone, earth or
water. So whilst a farmer or a fisherman might develop
extensive weathering, only a man who spent a lot of
time on a beach would gain that distinctively tanned
appearance.

THE SEVENTH SWORD

Given the distances between the villages, the application of Pythagoras' theorem will quickly establish the height of the triangle they form, treating any one of the lines as the base. If Rushock to Chaddesley is the base, the height of the triangle to Shenstone is one and one fifth miles. This makes the area of the triangle twenty-one twenty-fifths of a square mile. Then multiply the three sides together and divide by four times the area to get the distance to the central spot, and you'll discover that the distance is thirteen sixteenths of a mile.

THE WOOD MERCHANT

When Holmes told me what the police were missing, I found it unbelievable that it had not occurred to me as well. The wood-merchant was well tanned. It takes months to grow a big beard, during which time the skin of the face is shielded from the sun. If he had shaved such a facial adornment off so recently, his mouth and neck would be several shades lighter than the rest of his face.

THE DARK MARRIAGE

Holmes explained to me that the man had married a woman who had died. Afterwards, he married her sister. When he himself died, the sister was left a widow – making his original wife his widow's sister.

THE FOURTH LITERAL ODDITY

As it transpired, Holmes was driving at the syllables in the words. Scraunched and strengthed are both single-syllable words. At ten letters, they are the longest such in the English language, although I understand that the American word squirreled is also pronounced by them with a single syllable. It will always be a two-syllable word to my poor English brain. Io, by comparison, is the shortest possible two-syllable word, having as it does just two letters. I must confess to being rather taken with the word scraunched. It has a nice feel.

— ◆ —

PORT AND BRANDY

I was busily trying to juggle percentages and the such when Holmes pointed out that the two decanters would both contain exactly as much liquid as when they started. This meant that however much port had gone into the brandy would be exactly offset by the amount of brandy added to the port.

I tried his blend, and as he suggested, it was in fact a very engaging drink, albeit a potent one.

THE FIFTH MENTAL TRIAL

I managed to formulate an answer. If Holmes had less than the average number of coins, he had to bring the total average down. The average of sixty farthings across the three boys is twenty farthings each. There could not be a part-coin, so as Holmes' three coin deficit brought the average down exactly, and there were three boys, his contribution was effectively the same as removing one coin from each boy. So the average between the four was one less than it had been, or 19, and Holmes had 16 coins in his pocket.

I forestalled him before he could flip me a thrupenny bit too.

SQUARES

The solution to this challenge comprises the numbers 9, 81, 324 and 576.

STAMINA

It was the sweat that gave him away. In such temperatures, one single half-pint of water is not enough to keep a man sufficiently hydrated to permit such luxuries as sweating. Had I been less fatigued on arrival, I would have immediately recognised that my own perspiration had long since dried up. I'm not sure whether the chap ahead of me had cut out a large chunk of the course, or obtained a surfeit of water somewhere along the route, but either way, he'd broken the terms of the exercise.

THE FIFTH CURIOSITY

It is obviously bunk. The designation 'B.C.' was not even invented until the year 532 A.D., and when Henry I was the monarch, he was known simply as Henry. He did not gain his appellate 'I' until Henry II took the throne.

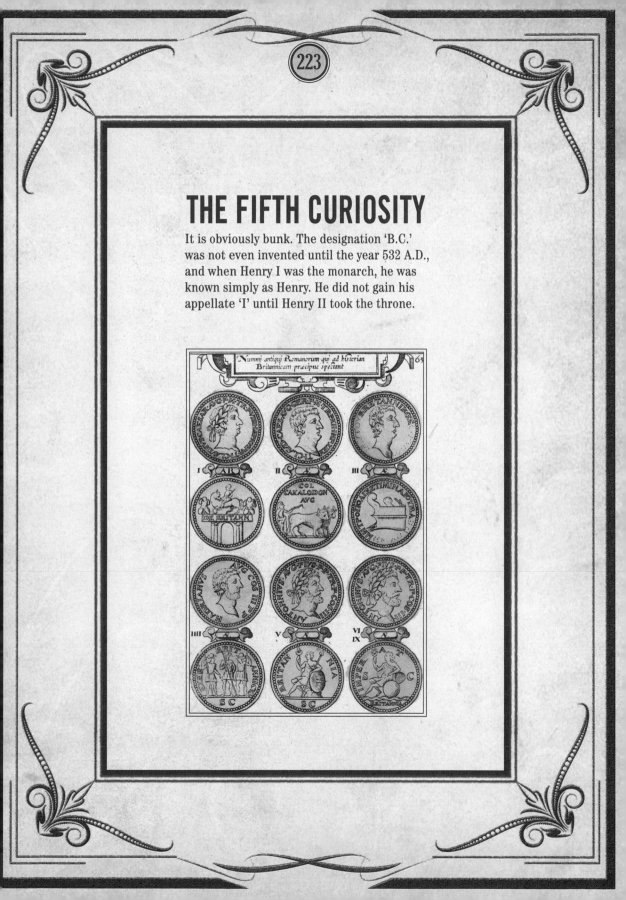

THE SECOND PORTMANTEAU

The image refers to none other than Windsor Castle,
Queen Victoria's preferred home when engaging in
Royal entertainments. The Queen herself is shown
sitting in a most comfortable chair, indicating that she
is both at home and at ease in this location. That alone
is enough to narrow the location down considerably.
The castle is sited on a small hill above the village of
Windsor, and apart from its own architecture, perhaps
its best-known feature is the Long Walk, a leafy parade
as illustrated, which stretches south for some three
miles from the castle gate.

FORTY-EIGHT

The next number with the same property is 1,680, where 1,681 is the square of 41, and 841 is the square of 29. The next after that is 57,120, and the one after is almost two million.

THE SHOREDITCH BANK JOB

"They are writers, old friend. This is a copy of their previous crime caper." Holmes tossed a lurid-looking novel onto the table. "They wanted the details of their story to be plausible. Their book was accepted for publication last week, and the constable who had assisted them with knowledge of proper procedure was fairly paid for his time and expertise."

THE DAY OF THE BOOK

During Shakespeare's lifespan, England used and kept the Julian calendar. Spain, however, changed to the Gregorian in 1582. The date of Shakespeare's death is recognised in accordance with the Julian calendar which he lived under, but if it is adjusted to the Gregorian calendar, it would actually fall on May 3rd. Cervantes died on April 23rd by the Gregorian calendar, 11 days before Shakespeare did.

THE CROSS OF ST. GEORGE

If you divide the flag into equal quarters, then the difference between the diagonal of this quarter-piece and half of its perimeter is the required width of the red cross. Pythagoras will tell us that the diagonal is 2½ feet, and in addition will confirm that half of the perimeter is 3½ feet. So the arm of the cross must be 1 foot wide.

THE SOMEWHAT CROOKED BUTLER

It is tempting to suggest that the jug would have to be 2½ gallons in size, but in fact that is not sufficient, as the second drawing will contain a certain amount of water in addition to ale. In fact, it has to be two gallons and ninety-three hundredths to get exactly to a fifty-fifty mix in two drawings.

CAMPANOLOGY

As there are just six possible arrangements of three items, it is not excessively tough:

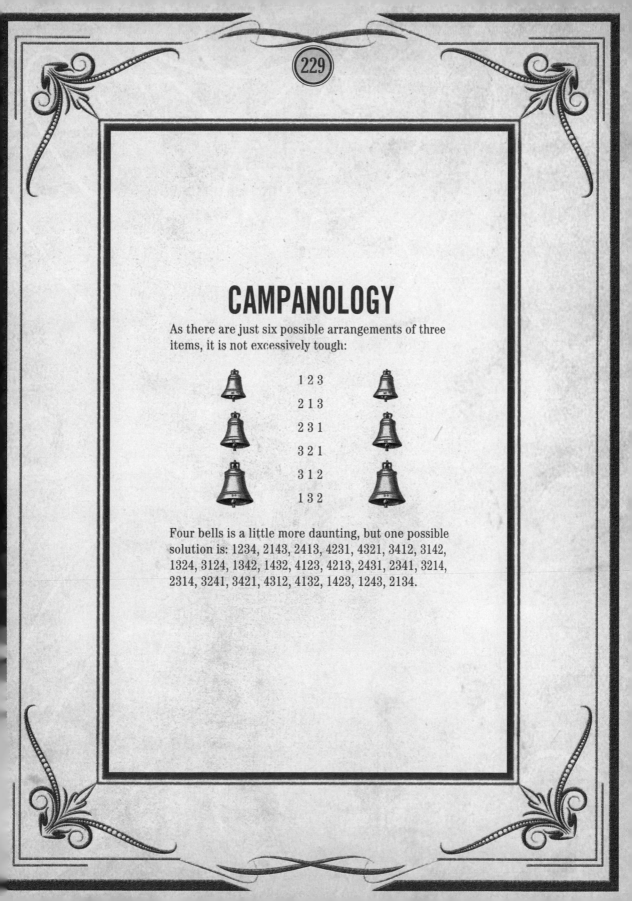

1 2 3
2 1 3
2 3 1
3 2 1
3 1 2
1 3 2

Four bells is a little more daunting, but one possible solution is: 1234, 2143, 2413, 4231, 4321, 3412, 3142, 1324, 3124, 1342, 1432, 4123, 4213, 2431, 2341, 3214, 2314, 3241, 3421, 4312, 4132, 1423, 1243, 2134.

C

There is a solution which requires just three operators.

If you do not have it yet, you might like to take this chance to look away.

No?

Still with me?

Very well. The answer is brilliant in its simplicity.
123 - 45 - 67 + 89 = 100.

THE HUDSON CLAN

Sally is Mrs. Hudson's third cousin once removed.
This means that Mrs. Hudson's great-grandmother
was the sister of Sally Shaw's great-great-
grandmother. Sally's grandmother – Mary, as it
transpired – would thus have been a second cousin
to Mrs. Hudson's mother Ada, as their grandmothers
were sisters. So moving back down the generations,
Mary was second cousin once removed to Mrs.
Hudson, and second cousin twice removed to her
son. Holmes was able to set her straight, but we were
neither of us any clearer on why she needed to know.

COUSIN JENNIFER

It took me a moment or two, which tickled Mrs.
Hudson greatly, but the answer did come to me
eventually. Cousin Jennifer was newly born, so
naturally could not do a thing for herself, nor walk
out of the hospital at the tender age of seven days.

THE FIFTH LITERAL ODDITY

Both of the primary words Holmes mentioned contain
the six vowel letters once and once only, in ascending
alphabetical order, without any repetition. It is my
belief that facetiously, at eleven letters, is the shortest
such word. Subcontinental, on the other hand, has all
five major vowels in reverse order, again once and once
alone.

I believe it to be the longest such, provided that
one discounts the noble efforts of uncomplimentary
because of the out of place 'y' at the end.

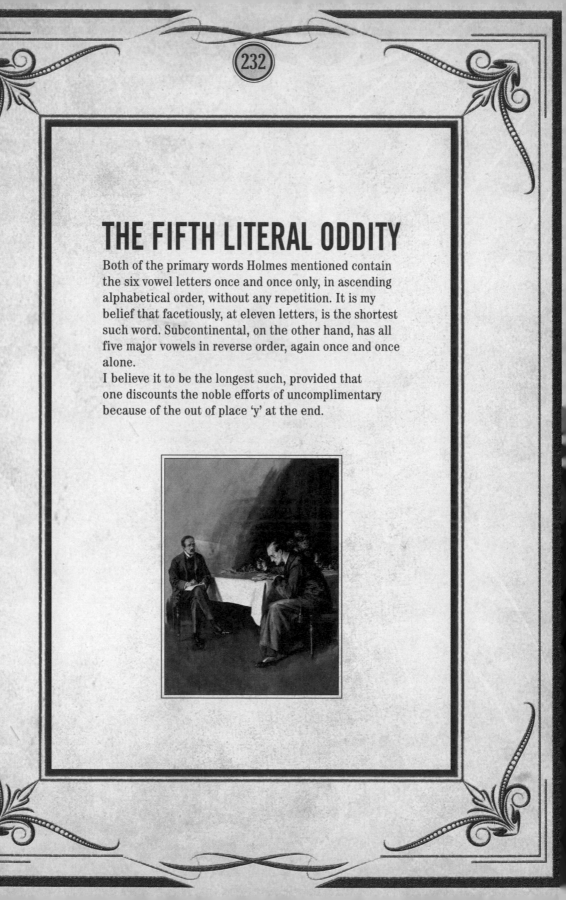

THE ABBOT

You know that there are five times as many women as men, so the best policy here is to start with 1 man, and work from there. 1 man means 5 women, for a total of 13 modia. That leaves 87 for 174 children, 180 people in total. Far too many. 3 men means 15 women, and 39 modia, but that's still 122 children, and 140 people. But you can see the progression – 2 more men means 40 less people. So the answer is 5 men, with 25 women and 70 children. That's a hundred people, using 15 + 50 + 35 = 100 modia of corn.

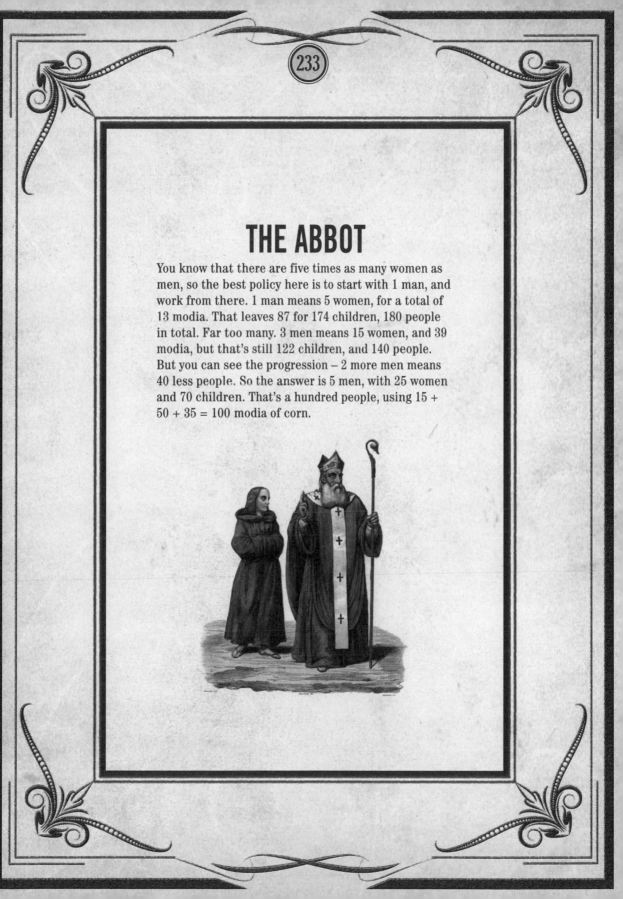

PART THREE

CUNNING

✳ ✳ ✳

THE STATUETTE

"Watson old chap, you'd best stick to medicine," Holmes said. "The two men were in cahoots. The pair pick a likely item. One buys it and talks up the value of its twin, and then the other sells it back again to the same dealer, at great profit. They split the proceeds, and when the poor dealer comes hoping to sell what he thinks is the companion piece, his original client has moved on. Instead of making £800, he has lost £200. The pair were only caught in their deception because they became greedy, and tried two such stings in London in too short a space of time."

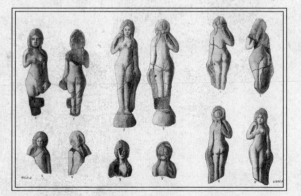

COLD HANDS

"There are two factors responsible for the cool effect of the vigorous breath. One is evaporation. As the air blows across your skin, higher-energy water molecules evaporate off. This reduces the average energy of the remaining molecules, and brings down their temperature, cooling you. This process occurs more rapidly with a harder breath, chiefly because the increased speed of the air encourages more of your sweat to make the leap to the gaseous state.

"The other, more minor, factor is gaseous expansion. As the breath comes from between your pursed lips, it spreads out from that tight position you had it in. The act of occupying a greater space reduces its temperature, for certain, somewhat abstract reasons. This means that the air actually is a little cooler."

DEDICATION

I am, of course, talking about clocks - ranging in number of components from hourglasses, with their myriad of sand grains, down to the good old sundial. Grandfather clocks can be far larger than a man, whilst some truly miniscule hourglasses are available.

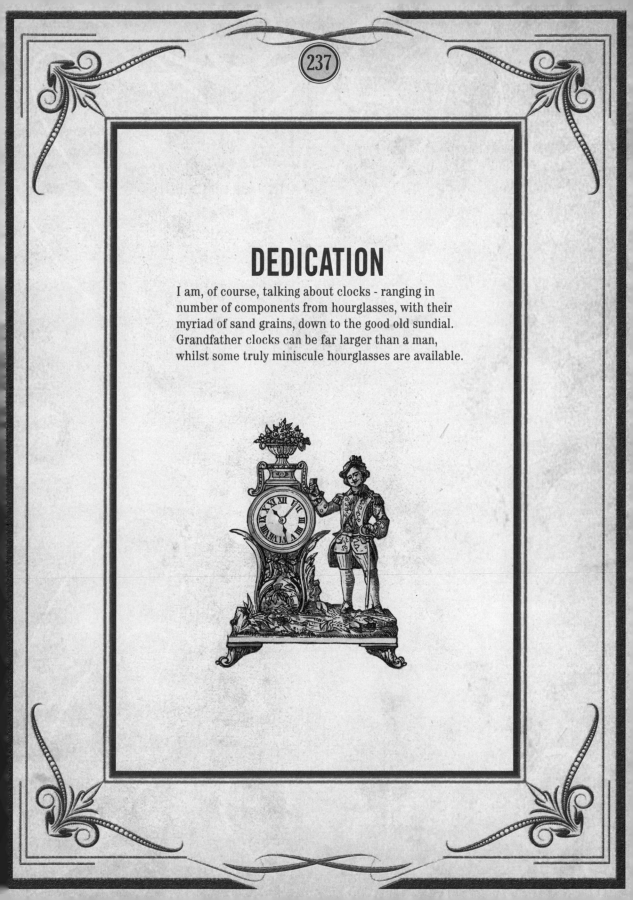

GRAINS OF SAND

The simple answer is that no, for the bulk of the time, the weight of the glass will not be affected. The missing weight from the falling sand is counterbalanced by the extra downward pressure from the grains which strike the bottom. There is a slight lessening of weight as the sand first starts to fall, before any has hit the floor, and a concomitant slight gain of weight at the end, when there is no sand remaining to start falling, but not all of it has landed yet.

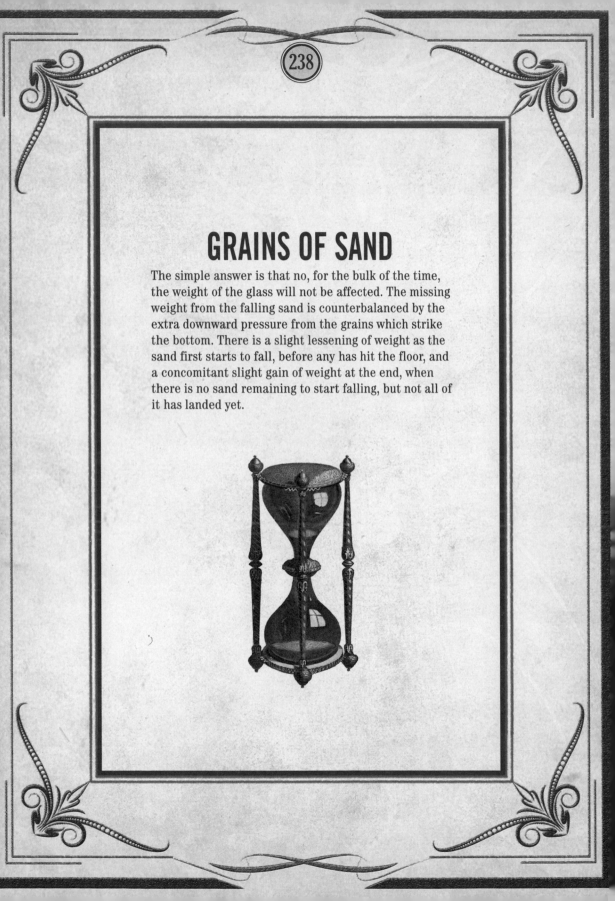

THE GREEN STONE

Although my friend's powers of deduction are utterly
beyond me, I was able to discern what he was getting
at on this occasion. The poison was in the ice of the
first drink they were served. Rebecca drank hers
quickly, before the ice had been given sufficient time
to melt, and escaped harm. His husband, in much
less of a hurry, lingered too long, and got a fatal dose.
The evident truth of this helped our client set aside a
measure of her guilt, I am happy to report, and allowed
her to begin grieving properly.

THE SIXTH CURIOSITY

Upon reflection, no, it is in fact a wild bilking. Two 6"
circles together are half as large as one 12" circle. Mrs.
Hudson should have paid half her usual sum.

THE CULT OF THE RED STAR

It turns out he was referring to the same man by each of those relationships. The victim's mother was the murderer's sister (father's brother-in-law). The victim had a brother, who had married the murderer's daughter (brother's father-in-law), and he himself had married the daughter of the murderer's brother (father-in-law's brother).

AFTERNOON

It can only be twenty-six minutes to six.

DIMPLES

"They contribute in two ways," Holmes informed me. "First, by making the surface of the ball irregular, they help trap the air that they fly through for longer. This reduces the wake that the ball leaves in the air, which in turn reduces the drag on it. Less drag, less deceleration, and the ball flies further. The other is due to the spin of the ball. Golf clubs impart backspin to the ball, and thanks to that backwards spin, the flow lines of the air around the ball are pushed downwards, effectively pushing the ball upwards, and greatly lengthening its distance. Without dimples, the air will tend to just scoot straight over the ball without being pushed."

SUFFOCATION

The question that Holmes asked was: "Did you see the time reflected in the hall mirror?" The poor maid gasped, and went as white as a sheet, because of course that was exactly what she had done. The nephew had left at 6:11, not at 5:49, and eventually the murderous fool confessed that he'd killed his aunt in desperation, as she was about to write him out of her will.

THE SIXTH LITERAL ODDITY

They are all words which have no repeated letters.
Being fifteen letters long, they each make use of more
than half of the alphabet. I was amused to note that
despite this, there are six letters which none of the
four encompasses.

THE SIXTH MENTAL TRIAL

The four are descended from each other in a straight
line. It is the only way to order the switching around.
George is Alfie's father, Fred is Alfie's son, and Harry is
Alfie's infant grandson.

WATCH OUT

"It's the difference in air pressure," Holmes informed me. "Higher up, the air is thinner. Makes it harder to breathe, but it also means that the air gives less resistance to the watch spring. This makes it run faster."

AFGHAN SHOT

Along one short side of the box, you can fit 85 balls, placed as 13 rows alternating 7 and 6 balls. The next layer above can fit twelve rows, again alternating, to give 78 balls. This pattern of layers can be repeated all along the length, to a total of 15 layers. Summing these up, 8 layers of 85 balls and 7 layers of 78 gives us a full crate of 1,226 balls.

THE DINNER TABLE

There is only one pair of solutions that will give each man new partners every time, and yet still keep George 3 seats away around the table, and Bill just two seats distant. These are as follows: Alfie, Fred, Bill, Don, George, Eric, Charlie; and Alfie, Eric, Bill, George, Charlie, Fred, Don.

THE BICYCLE

If you process through the years and consider the ratios, the answer will quickly become apparent. Three times 13 is 39, seven years out; a year later, three times 14 is 42, five years off the mother's new age of 47. So for each year that passes, the time to close the gap shortens by two years. If you stick with jumping whole years however, the gap will go from 1 year to -1 year, so you need to use a half-year to get the gap to exactly zero. At 15, it is 3 years difference, at 16 it is 1 year, so at 16½ the girl will be exactly a third of her mother's age, which will be 49½. The girl has to wait 3½ years.

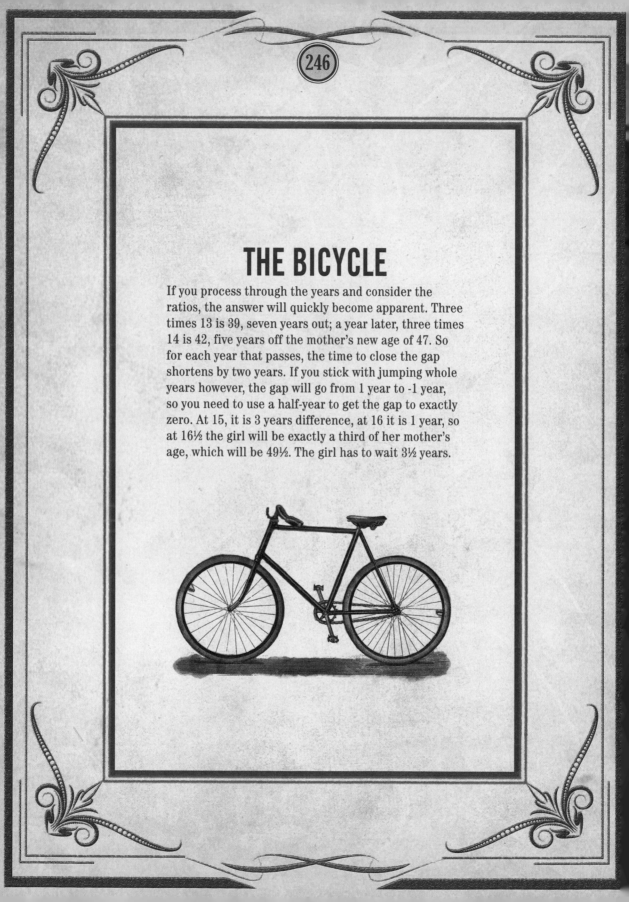

HIGHLAND FLING

"It's as plain as the hairs on your head, Watson. The supposed witch packed the bell with snow before her dramatic entrance. It stopped the bell sounding, and then either shook loose thanks to the exertions of the bell-ringer, or melted away in the intervening time. I'd need to check in person to see which, and I have no intention of doing any such thing. Either way, the addled locals failed to notice the obvious explanation, turning instead to the most arrant foolishness."

BIG SQUARES

You will discover that the smallest possible nine-digit square number which makes use of each of the digits once and once alone is 139,854,276.

THE SEVENTH LITERAL ODDITY

To my surprise, it turns out that there are just three words ending in -bt, doubt, debt and redoubt. Their commonality fooled me into the assumption that if I could think of three off the top of my head there had to be many more, but it is not the case. Likewise, there are just three standard words ending with -gry – angry, hungry, and the reasonably obscure puggry, the latter being a light head-scarf worn over a hat as additional solar protection.

THE SWITCH

It is an interesting fact that the number of pairs of times when the hands of a clock switch exact position can be calculated from the hour as such: consider how many whole hours there are from the current hour to midnight, and subtract one. The current hour is 3, so there nine hours to midnight, and our value is eight. Then take your value, and add the whole numbers together, in order, from one, until you reach the same number as your value. If the value was two, you would add 1 and 2, for a total of 3; but ours is 8. Adding these, $1 + 2 + 3 + 4 + 5 + 6 + 7 + 8$ gives 36, the correct answer.

THE CIRCUS

The murdered performer had taken the magician's assistant as a sweetheart, but he had a lethally jealous rival – the musical conductor. The trapeze act used the musical score to provide the necessary split-second timing. Holmes had heard the conductor change the timing of the music, speeding it up just enough so that when it came to make his dashing leap, the trapeze artist was out of position. He leapt too soon, trusting the music, and crashed to his death.

THE THIRD PORTMANTEAU

The solution is that the image points to the Palace of Westminster, commonly referred to as the Houses of Parliament. The elegant building represents the House of Lords, our parliament of inherited peers. The rougher one represents the House of Commons, our elected representatives, although I must hasten to point out that our parliamentarians are to be considered common only in the sense of not being Peers of the Realm. The two Houses are ineluctably intertwined in the government of Britain, as the rope indicates. The arguing men indicate the political divisions in British public life, which ever invite raucous debate – often, I'd wager, such disagreements are more for the look of the thing than from any great variance of principle, but still, disagreements they remain. The pole with the carriage clock represents the mighty St. Stephen's clock tower which so characterises the view of central London. In the image, this is overshadowed by the bell; this reflects the fact that the tower itself is overshadowed by Big Ben – its most famous occupant, the great bell which rings out the hour.

URCHINS

Every lad will walk next to every other lad once, so will form eight pairs. Four of those pairs will be formed two at a time, when he is in the middle of the three, and the other four singly, when he is on the end of a group. Therefore he will require six outings to walk with everyone once.

THE MEADOW OF DEATH

As Holmes pointed out, the lack of any signs of human agency in the couple's demise suggested some sort of environmental factor. We know that they were not poisoned, so toxic gas is ruled out. The lack of broken limbs, the proximity to the village, and their being hand in hand together all suggest that they were not in notable distress prior to their deaths, so that whatever killed them was very sudden. By Holmes' confession, he had made no mention of the length of time that they had been dead. As it transpired, they had been out walking in the winter, and had been completely buried in a sudden slide of snow. They had remained there, hidden, all winter, only to be discovered after the thaw had come.

THE EGG

Holmes proposed that the answer lay in Mr. Darwin's theory of natural selection. Birds, Holmes observed, habitually breed in lofty places – trees, cliffs, and the like. In such a situation, an egg which was able to roll any great distance would surely be at a disadvantage. By contrast, the oddly unbalanced shape which is so familiar to us all will roll on a swiftly curving path, making it a safer design.

THE EIGHTH LITERAL ODDITY

The two are amongst the longest English words which are anagrams of each other. Furthermore, and even more impressively, they do not share any letter-pairs in common, neither is any letter in one of the words in the same position in the other. That is quite a feat, in a fourteen-letter anagram pair.

This may be compared to the admittedly longer anagram pair of conservationalists and conversationalists, which at eighteen letters, are the longest non-scientific English anagram pair, but where the only difference is the rather trivial transposition of the 's' and the 'v'.

GOLD

The box is 100x100" square, and 11" deep. The floor of
the box contains layers of eight by nine slabs, leaving
a one inch gap on the side. Eleven of these layers will
fill the box to the top, accounting for 792 of the slabs.
That leaves eight slabs to go in on their edge in a space
100 inches by 11 inches – one exact row of eight slabs
lengthways.

STONES

The distances would rapidly increase to the ludicrous,
of course, particularly having to go back and forth each
time. In fact, for fifty stones, the distance travelled
to collect them all, in yards, would be 50 x 49 x 99 / 3
yards, and 80,850 yards is very nearly 46 miles.

HUDSONS TANGLED

When Katie was three times as old as Alison, Katie was 16½ and Alison 5½ (11 years younger). Then we get 49½ for the age Alison will be when she is three times as old as Katie was then. When Katie was half this she was 24¾. And at that time Alison must have been 13¾ (11 years younger). Or, in the other direction, Katie is (27½) twice as old as Alison was (13¾) when Katie was half as old (24¾) as Alison will be (49½) when Alison is three times as old (49½) as Katie was (16½) when Katie was (16½) three times as old as Alison (5½).

So the age of Katie to that of Alison must be in the proportion 5 to 3, and as the sum of their ages is 44, Katie is 27½ and Alison 16½.

THE SEVENTH CURIOSITY

It took me a long moment to recollect t hat Herod had ordered only boy children slain. All the feet would have belonged to boys.

— ◦ — ◦ —

FENCING

"That sort of tone can only be caused from a flat, dull noise by broken reflections of sound," Holmes explained. "You would need to be near a set of railings of some sort, or something of a similar structure with many small bars close together in parallel. Each one reflects a tiny fraction of the sound, but at a precisely staggered interval, being slightly further away than the last. It is this effect which causes the apparent ringing."

THE SOHO PIT

The man is going twice as deep as he has done so far, so when finished, the hole will be a total of three times its present depth. The current depth of the hole has to be less than his height, and, when finished, greater than his height but less than twice that. Within those bounds, the only solution is that the hole is currently 3ft 6 deep, and when finished, will be 10ft 6.

THE SEVENTH MENTAL TRIAL

Alfie has two brothers, and four sisters. With three men and four women, each woman has three of each sex of sibling, and each man has two brothers and four sisters. Bill, by comparison, is from a family of five. Each of the brothers has one brother and three sisters, and each of the sisters has two of each. So Alfie, with two brothers, has one more than Bill does.

THE HANGED MAN

As Holmes was so fond of saying, when the impossible had been discounted, the improbable, no matter how unlikely, had to be the truth. It was impossible that the killer had left the room so securely fastened, so he had to still be in the room, and that meant the death was a suicide. Holmes' fingers were wet after touching the carpet because the artist used a block of ice to stand on when fastening his noose to the ceiling, wearing boots against the cold. Then he kicked the block down flat and died, determined to leave one last riddle. The ice later melted, but the carpet was still damp.

HAPPY FAMILY

"From what we are told, we know that Barney's age is twice Amelia's, and Charlotte's presence brings their combined total to twice Barney's. This means that together, Amelia and Charlotte combined are worth four times Amelia's age alone, and so Charlotte is three times Amelia's age.

"Later, we are told that Barney and Daniel together total twice Amelia and Charlotte, but Emily's addition reverses this. Again, this tells us that Emily is three times the combined age of Amelia and Charlotte. We know Emily is 21, so Amelia and Charlotte together are 7 years old. Dividing seven into quarters, for Charlotte's age is three times that of Amelia's, we can discern that Amelia is 1¾, whilst Charlotte is 5¼. From here, it is simple. Barney is twice Amelia's age, or 3½, and Daniel's age – by the same logic we used for the girls – has to be three times Barney's, or 10½.

"So Amelia is 1¾, Barney is 3½, Charlotte is 5¼, Daniel is 10½, and Emily, as we know already, is 21 years of age."

THE BARN

"I'll put you out of your misery, Inspector. It is a simple enough matter. Your fellow rode to the barn during the snowstorm. The snowfall obliterated the signs of his passing. He then turned the shoes round on his horse, so they were pointing in the wrong direction.

"Without inspecting the barn myself, I cannot say whether he found the tools he needed on site, and was struck by inspiration, or whether he brought them with him with confusion in mind all along. If the latter, he may have removed the horse's shoes before the evening's escapade began. Either way, it is no great matter to put them on back to front.

"Then, with his horse suitably attired, he waited until the snow stopped, and rode off, boldly leaving a clear trail that would be sure to fox his pursuit."

A HEARTY DROP

The first action is to fill the pail, and then fill the jar from the pail. Alfie then quaffs the contents of the pail. There are now 7 pints in the barrel, 3 pints in the jar, and 2 pints in Alfie.

Next, the contents of the jar are poured back into the pail, and the jar is filled again from the barrel. That leaves 4 pints in the barrel, which Bill grabs happily, and three pints in each vessel.

The jar is poured into the pail until the pail is full, leaving 1 pint inside the jar, and five in the pail. Charlie drinks the pint in the jar. Then the jar is filled again from the pail, leaving two pints inside it. Charlie takes the jar, for his four pints in total, and Alfie gets the pail, with his remaining two pints. The men can then take more time over their remaining drinks, although Bill has some catching up to do.

PART FOUR

FIENDISH

✳ ✳ ✳ ✳

THE EIGHTH MENTAL TRIAL

It might be tempting to divide the money up according to the amount of oil each man had before the operation, 8 and 5 farthings, but that would be unfair to Alfie. Thirteen pints of oil are split between the three men. That leaves each man with 4 and 1/3 pints. Bill has lost just 2/3 of a pint of oil; the bulk of the donation has come from Alfie, who has lost 3 and 2/3.

To discover a fair breakdown, first think of the entire donation in terms of thirds of a pint. 3 pints is 9 third-pints, as any publican will tell you, so Alfie has lost 11 thirds to Bill's 2. The fair division of the money then is 11 farthings to Alfie, and 2 to Bill.

IN PARIS

As Holmes eventually pointed out, the only two rational possibilities were either that the woman was demented, or that the entire hotel staff were colluding against her. The former option, whilst neat, would hardly have occasioned his presenting the matter to me in such a manner.

As it happened, the staff were indeed colluding. The brother had been diagnosed with severe typhoid fever during the night, and was immediately whisked away to a small, quiet hospice outside the city. Terrified that news of the lethally infectious disease might panic the World's Fair visitors and lead to a scandalous financial disaster, the manager had the room sealed and disguised, and briefed all the staff to remain resolute in the face of the lady's questioning.

POP POP

"It is a matter of air pressure," said Holmes. "The heat of the boiler turns the water inside it to steam. Steam takes up much more space that water does, so the pressure of this steam bubble forces the water in the bottom of the exhaust to be expelled in a jet. The boat is pushed forwards by the force of this jet. The relative coolness of the exhaust pipe – compared to the boiler – almost immediately causes the steam bubble to condense back into water. This creates an empty vacuum, because the mechanism is closed off from the air, and the water is sucked back up the exhaust to its position prior to the beginning of the expansion. It is then heated back to steam, and the cycle repeats."

"That's all well and good," I replied, "but why doesn't the second part of the operation cancel out the first?"

"Ah, that's the clever bit. When the water is expelled, it is pushed out in one direction alone, all its force concentrated, so the boat accelerates off in the other direction. But when it is drawn back in, it comes in from all around the end of the pipe, in every direction, so the force is all spread out, and the boat cannot react against it. If you wish a demonstration, trying to extinguish a candle flame by sucking air rather than blowing it. Do mind not to burn your lips, however!"

EVASION

The simplest approach is to round up the combined age a little, to 50. Then it can be seen fairly easily that if the man is 30 and the woman 20, when he was 20, she would have been 10, and he would have been twice her age.

The real sum is not quite so neat, but now we know the approximate divisions, it is reasonably straightforward to ascertain that he is twenty-nine and two fifths, and she is nineteen and three-fifths. When he was the latter age, she was half that, at nine and four fifths.

SIX-SIDED DICE

Consider 1 die first of all. The 4, 5 and 6 can be discounted, as their positions are fixed by the earlier numbers. Then the 1 can be marked on any of 6 faces. That leaves 4 faces for the 2 to occupy, and 2 faces for the three. Multiplying these out, there are 48 options for marking one die. Each subsequent die can be marked independently of the other two, so the grand total of possible marking schemes for three six-sided dice is 110,592.

THE NINTH LITERAL ODDITY

I must admit that I was unable to find an answer until
Holmes suggests that I write the words down using only
capital letters, to wit CHECKBOOK and EXCEEDED.
Then it became clear that they were composed
entirely of letters that possessed horizontal symmetry
as capitals. If you placed a mirror over the top half
of the word and reflected the bottom half with it, it
would be unchanged. I dare say you could contrive the
word 'COOKBOOKED', or some similar chimera, but I
personally feel that would be something of a dodge.

THE DICTIONARY

With care, it proved possible to arrange the books so that the fifth protruded entirely over the table. The trick lies in counting back from the top book. It is possible to push one single book up to half-way out without having it topple. To then extend the second book over a third, one can go just half the distance of the one above. To extend that third, half as much again, and so on. Proceeding in this manner, after extending the fifth book, the top volume is just a little clear of the base.

Holmes assured me that there was no theoretical maximum as to how far clear the top book may be extended. I politely informed him that I believed him implicitly, and would be happy to watch if he was minded to provide a demonstration, but that I was not inclined to physically test the maxim any further. No such demonstration has yet been forthcoming.

THE EIGHTH CURIOSITY

I was astounded to hear that it would raise the girdle by very nearly a full yard – approximately 19/20ths, if you wish to be more precise.

THE FISH MURDER

"What blade could a man leave behind in an enemy's neck, yet have it vanish into thin air within minutes, Watson?"

I had to confess my bafflement.

"Ice, dear fellow. A spike of ice. Easily prepared and brought in with the ice packing the day's catch. It would stay strong enough to create a piercing wound for several minutes, but would be completely gone in short order, particularly if left within the heat of flesh. Weir was unlucky with the timing of the patrol, but by running, ensured the constables were distracted long enough for the blade to melt away."

THE BOX

From the extension of Pythagoras' theorem, it can be seen that the areas of the top and side multiplied together and then divided by the area of the end give the square of the length. 120 x 96 / 80 gives us 144, so the box is 12 inches in length. From there, it is simple to see that it is 10 inches broad, and 8 inches deep.

SHEEP

"At no point did I tell you that the pens had to be empty before you began, Watson. If one of the pens contains a sheep already, the matter is trivial. I do not present this problem to make sport with you, but to highlight that it is vital to look for solutions which are beyond the obvious."

THE FOURTH PORTMANTEAU

As I eventually managed to deduce, the image refers to Hyde Park. The river Serpentine is the dominant feature of the park, hence the coils of water ending in the head of a snake. The park was the site of the first World's Fair in 1851, the Great Exhibition, which was housed in the great Crystal Palace, which was later rebuilt, in modified form, in Penge. The park is also host to Speaker's Corner, where by tradition any man or woman may go to freely speak his mind, represented by the wild-tempered fellow on the box. It is perhaps an irony that Speaker's Corner is just a few yards away from the site of the infamous Tyburn Tree, the three-beamed gallows which took the lives of London's condemned for so many centuries.

GET A HAT

It should be clear that one person with one hat to choose can never be mistaken, two people can get it wrong in just one manner, and three people in just two. In fact, the general rule is that for each increase in the number of people, you need to multiply the previous result by the new total of persons. When that new total of persons is even, you must add 1 to your product, and when it is odd, you must remove one, to make allowance for the fact that an odd number of people have their options slightly restricted.

By calculating through, it will be found that seven men can get the wrong hats in 1,854 different ways. If you wanted to know just the number of all possible different ways the hats could be distributed, that would be 1 x 2 x 3 x 4 x 5 x 6 x 7, or 5,040.

NEPHEWS

"It's quite elementary, my dear fellow. If two men each marry the (possibly widowed) mother of the other, and both father a son upon their new wives, then those sons will be both uncle and nephew to each other, as each will be the brother of the other's father. There are other ways to achieve the relationship too, but that is the most straight-forward."

THE NINTH MENTAL TRIAL

After I had pondered the matter for a while, Holmes came to my rescue. "You can do it in just two operations," he assured me. "Divide the coins into three piles of three. Place two upon the scales and compare them. If one side is lighter, that pile contains the fake; if the two are equal, the set-aside pile holds it. Clear the scale, and take the pile with the fake. Now place any two of the coins upon the scales and again compare. If one is lighter, it is the fake; if they are the same, it is the held-over coin. The method is infallible."

EQUITY

The solution which most readily presents itself to me is this:

$$79 + 5 + 1/3 = 84 + 2/6$$

I do not believe that it can be done without the use of fractions.

TWENTY THOUSAND LEAGUES

"It's a matter of buoyancy, old friend. While the device remained surrounded by water on all sides, the pressure of that water would be pushing in all directions, including upwards. Therefore it would not present too great an impediment to progress. So long as it did not crush the submersible like an egg, anyway. However, if the machine was allowed to land, this could drive the water out from underneath the device. Suddenly there would be no upward pressure, just downwards. Lacking the most incredible engines, the machine would be pinned in place, like a butterfly in a case – a death sentence to be sure."

THE SHOREDITCH BANK

The reason for the apparent lapse in security was clearly obvious as soon as we entered the office. The clever villains had prepared an accurate depiction of the safe, somewhat larger than the real thing, and propped it up so as to appear, from the door, as if nothing was wrong. They were then able to work on opening the safe, and when the guards came past and looked in, everything appeared to be in order. The deception would have been more obvious if the office had been brightly lit, but as it was, it was more than sufficient to buy the thieves the time they needed. Even Holmes seemed a little impressed by their ingenuity.

MARKHAM

"There are two lines of approach to solving this problem. One is the elliptical. You may notice, on the side table, a bottle of pills near to the decanter of Scotch. Markham was ill, and as the widow did not mention it, we can assume she did not know. Furthermore, it bespeaks a certain bleakness of outlook when a man keeps his medication next to his hard liquor.

"The other approach is more direct. The room was sealed from the inside, and we are told it is impossible that the intruder escaped unseen. It is within reason that both widow and maid may be in cahoots, but if they allowed an assailant to escape, how did they seal the room back up without being caught within it?

"No Watson, the matter is far more straightforward. If it is impossible that anyone escaped, then the unlikely must be true, and the killer is still in there – dead. Markham's prognosis must have been stark enough that he could not bear to suffer through it. He locked the room, staged the argument, and took his own life. If you look through his paperwork, I have no doubt you'll find a life insurance policy that pays handsomely in case of murder, but not at all when it comes to suicide. Let the police seek their unlikely suspect however. I see no need to burden the widow any further."

MONTENEGRO

The suitable pairs would be 5 and 9 for one player, and 13 and 15 for the other. You can make 5 in six ways, and 9 in twenty-five, for a total of 31 chances; and you can make 13 in 21 ways, and 15 in 10 ways, also for 31 chances. In any given throw with these numbers, there will be a 1/7th chance of attaining victory.

WORDPLAY

Given that there are no English words without a vowel – Y is not in our range of options, remember – then our possible maximum number of words is restricted to the groups that contain one of these four. A further restriction is that there is no common English word formed from just three vowels. Even if we had a U available, I.O.U. is an abbreviation, not a word. So with that in mind, there are a maximum of 22 non-repetitive groups that contain at least one consonant and at least one vowel. If 'Jek' or its derivatives were words, it would be possible to attain that, but as they are not, the maximum practical is 21:

ALE	FOE	HOD	BGN
CAB	HEN	JOG	KFM
HAG	GEM	MOB	BFH
FAN	KIN	JEK	DFL
JAM	HIM	GCL	LJH
AID	JIB	FCJ	NJD
OAK	FIG	HCK	MLN
BED	OIL	MCD	BLK
ICE	CON		DGK

WIMBLEDON COMMON

The cabbie reacted so violently because his passenger gave his own home address as a destination. He had long suspected his wife of being engaged in an illicit affair, so when a perfect stranger asked to be taken to his own home, at a time when he himself ought to be safely out of the way, the man snapped. Instead of taking the visitor to his home, he took him out into the park and slaughtered him. Under French law, it is sometimes permissible for a jealous lover to be treated leniently for murder due to a temporary fit of insanity inflamed by the passions.

THE TENTH MENTAL TRIAL

"Your sign is white. If any man saw both of the black signs – Bill, let us say – he would know his own had to be white, and he would immediately step forward. Because he does not do so, Alfie can thus be certain that you and he do not between have both the black signs. So far, so good. Now, if you had a black sign, Alfie could be sure that his sign was white, because he knows you are not both wearing black, so he would be able to step forward. However, he does not do so. This can only mean that he sees a white sign on your back as well. Of course, any of the three of you could use parallel logic to arrive at the same conclusion, so it becomes a race of the wits as to which of you gets there first."

MOST IRREGULAR

If you try various whole year ages for the lad and work out whether the answers match the conditions, you'll find that you overshoot and undershoot between 9 and 8.

If Wiggins is nine, Father Anthony is 36, and Father Gary is 48. That would make David 16, but nine years ago, four times David's age would have been 28, not Father Anthony's 27, a difference of 1 year too much.

If Wiggins is eight, Father Anthony is 32, and Father Gary is 44. That would make David 14 2/3. Nine years ago, four times David's age would have been 22 2/3, but Father Anthony would have been 23, a difference of 1/3 of a year too little.

The discrepancies are 1/3 one side, and 3/3 the other side – a total of 4/3 of inaccuracy. This means that Wiggin's age lies between 8 and 9 in the same ratio of 1 past 8, and 3 before nine – or 8¼. Father Anthony is 33, and Father Gary is 45. David is 15, and nine years ago would have been 6, whilst Father Anthony was 24; and as 6 times 4 is 24, the ages match.

CARL BLACK

"Arson is a mark of desperation in an otherwise sober man," Holmes said. "I believe the root cause to be the kidnapping. Black had always been a flamboyant spender, and given the state of the company, it seems likely he had been embezzling. The partner, Robbins, would have needed a lever to move Black with, so I suspect he had discovered the embezzlement. Either way, between them they hatched a kidnap plot, and staged that business with the supposed Serbians. The insurance paid a hefty sum, Black departed quietly – and without scandal. The company finances improved markedly, which I assume was the combined benefit of the end of the embezzlement and the surreptitious slow feeding back in of the ransom money. All was well until Black got himself killed. Robbins felt that he couldn't take the risk that Black might have retained some sort of incriminatory document regarding the kidnapping amongst his effects, and panicked. It will all come out as the arson trial proceeds, mark my words."

A MATTER OF TIME

"The trick, dear fellow, is to make sure the two sticks are not touching, and light both ends of one, and just one end of the other. The stick burning from both ends will burn out in 30 minutes, whilst the second stick is still half-way through. At that point, light the other end of the second stick, and it will burn out in 15 minutes, for a total of 45 minutes."

THE FAULTY WATCH

It is a curious fact that the hands of a clock meet in their regular journey exactly every $65\frac{5}{11}$ minutes. So if my watch hands are meeting every 64 minutes, my watch is fast, and is gaining almost one and a half minutes every hour.

THE FINAL PORTMANTEAU

A pretty riddle, this one. It was the trees and plants that first set me on the right track. They are all different, and arranged with precision. Where would you find a wide variety of both trees and plants, precisely arranged? The most obvious answer would be to look in a herbarium. With that decided, it was only a matter of time before my mind turned to the Royal Botanic Gardens at Kew, and all the pieces fell into place.

Occupying 120 hectares of gardens and glasshouses, Kew Gardens holds the largest herbarium on Earth, as well as a vast collection of living specimens. Their habitats include the impressive Palm House and Temperate House, respectively the first and largest wrought-iron glass-houses in existence. The former's beguiling curves are hinted at in the glass-house shown picture, as is the scale of the latter. The Alpine House provides a cold environment for chill-weather plants. The Great Pagoda is one of the Gardens' more impressive follies, and for some time was the largest Chinese-style building in Europe.

The last piece of the puzzle is the 'farmer King' - King George III, God rest his soul. 'Farmer George' was a passionate agriculturalist, and he carried out several trials and adjustments at Kew. This even included a brave plan to strengthen British sheep by crossbreeding them with stolen specimens from Spain's famous, and well guarded, Merino flocks.

THE LADIES OF MORDEN

To get an answer which works effectively, you have to go through the players cyclically. Once that is understood, it becomes a matter of finding suitable starting places for each column at the beginning, and descending from there.

1.   A B vs I L   E J vs G K   F H vs C D
2.   A C vs J B   F K vs H L   G I vs D E
3.   A D vs K C   G L vs I B   H J vs E F
4.   A E vs L D   H B vs J C   I K vs F G
5.   A F vs B E   I C vs K D   J L vs G H
6.   A G vs C F   J D vs L E   K B vs H I
7.   A H vs D G   K E vs B F   L C vs I J
8.   A I vs E H   L F vs C G   B D vs J K
9.   A J vs F I   B G vs D H   C E vs K L
10. A K vs G J   C H vs E I   D F vs L B
11. A L vs H K   D I vs F J   E G vs B C

THE FINAL CURIOSITY

Although the effect is vanishingly small for a billiard table, to remain perfectly level for the players, it would have to follow the curvature of the Earth. If it were perfectly level, it would be closest to the Earth at its centre point, and the balls would all roll to the middle.

GROUPS

There are in fact two solutions to the problem. These are: 4 x 1,738 = 6,952 and 4 x 1,963 = 7,852. In both cases, all nine digits are used just once.

THE EGGTIMER'S COMPANION

There are only two sets of four numbers totalling 100 which have the squares of their lesser three numbers summing equal to the square of the larger. Thus Mr. Southwell is 39, his wife 34, his daughter 14, and his son 13, whilst Mr. Adams is 42, his wife 40, his daughter 10 and his son 8.

THE FINAL MENTAL TRIAL

The answer is 17. As I finally realised, the numbers are in increasing length when spelled out fully as words. Two has 3 letters, five has 4, and so on, up to fourteen with eight digits. The only number with nine digits that is less than twenty is seventeen.

CONES

"It is a general rule in this instance," Holmes later informed me, "that the greatest volume may be produced by cutting at just one third of the maximum height."